FOOTBALL

Mysteries Revealed
for the Feminine Fan

Understanding and Enjoying the Game

Janet Benner

Dear Susay,
Hope you
enjoy —
Janet Benner,
October, 1995

FOOTBALL: MYSTERIES REVEALED FOR THE FEMININE FAN
Understanding and Enjoying the Game

Copyright ©1995 by Janet Benner.

Published by: Joelle Publishing
    P.O. Box 91229
    Santa Barbara, CA 93190

Printed in the United States of America

Library of Congress Catalog Card Number: 95-77387

ISBN: 0-942723-15-5

DEDICATION

This book is lovingly dedicated to the memory of my son Kenneth Loryn Wells Smyth for whom the game of football was a source of great pleasure.

ACKNOWLEDGMENTS

I'm pretty much convinced that people rarely read the acknowledgments, which is too bad because it is such a nice tribute to the people who help make books happen. Nonetheless, I want to thank and acknowledge those who helped me. I will attempt to be brief.

Special thanks to Don Carlson, National Football League Side Judge #39, for taking time out of a busy schedule to read the manuscript and for setting me straight on the very latest rule changes. His help was invaluable.

Coach Uncle Marino Rosellini helped with ideas through endless discussions, read the manuscript to let me know where I was wrong, and enthusiastically supported the project. Without his expertise, the technical aspects would have been impossible.

Thanks to my son, Paul, who is so knowledgeable that he probably should be a coach, and who gave me excellent advice on difficult questions. Thanks to my daughter, Rachel, who through the years has enjoyed the game of football with me, making it all that much more fun.

John Zant, the Sports Section Editor and excellent writer for the *Santa Barbara News Press* helped with obscure information.

Marilyn Scott and Janet Ellman were my able editors. Their enthusiasm and encouragement were definitely appreciated.

The very clever cover design is a product of Robert Howard Design in Fort Collins, Colorado.

Norman Russell Design ably provided the interior book design and the illustrations. Since Norman is also my life partner, he lived through all the doubts and questions, offering answers, support, caring and love.

Thanks to B & B Copy for assistance with the illustrations.

Thanks to my office staff for being supportive throughout.

Thanks to Cynthia Maez, Holly Walton, Sharon Chessmar and Virginia Rosellini for willingly taking time to preview and comment on the manuscript from the female point of view

Lastly, I'd like to acknowledge the millions of women who bravely put aside their bafflement over the game of football every fall, and attempt to become one with the flow.

CONTENTS

PREFACE

I've just been reading *Men Are From Mars, Women Are From Venus*. As a student of the psychological, sociological, and political workings of we humans, I have avoided the notion that men and women are elementally different. I don't care for stereotyping; pigeonholing people or groups. These stereotypes act as a kind of social prison that prevent individuals and groups from being different from what their particular pigeonhole dictates. But I chuckled as I read *Men Are From Mars* because of how John Gray nailed so perfectly the way my significant other and I talk to each other. The reason I bring this other book up must be obvious. Maybe it is that football is a sport for men and women just generally find it unpleasant.

But, I'm convinced that the best of us all are a balance between the male and female of our species. Doesn't that open doors? And a cheer or two for my particular heros (heroines) Shirley Muldowney and Lynn St. James, both race car drivers.

I want the reader to know at the outset that I'm not a coach, nor am I an official, nor have I ever been a player on an organized football team with a coach and all the *accoutrement*. Which is to say, this is less a technical book than a spectator's book. The information that I do give I hope to be correct. There are times, however, when I question my own information and either don't know where to find the answer, or don't feel it's important to spend that much time on that particular point. If I'm not certain about some detail, I'll let you know.

Generally, the information in this book surrounds learning how to enjoy the game as I have through the years. If you want to become an expert, you'll have to research further, get the *NFL Rule Book*, as I kept saying I was going to do but never did. You could hang out with coaches and players if they'll let you. And read. There is lots to read. Most of it is technical and boring - not fun to read unless you really are an "armchair quarterback." Which is the real reason I have written *Football*. *Pursuing being a fan of football should be fun and not taken too awfully seriously.*

When I was reading for this book, titles like *A Payroll to Meet: A Story of Greed, Corruption and Football at SMU*, and *The Death of An American Game*, and *The Hundred Yard Lie* jumped off the shelf at me. I was surprised that the library had so many negative books about football.

But football players tend to create their own negative press. O.J. Simpson is on trial for murdering his ex-wife. The hype that surrounds the trial has brought into focus the possibility that the violence on the field of play is extended into the homes of many pro football players. I was dismayed when I heard on a TV news program that in the last seven years, 141 football players have been arrested for spousal abuse. I was the Director of a battered women's shelter and I have seen the hideous swollen bruises on the faces and bodies of battered women. A young woman was murdered by her husband during my tenure. It is an unspeakable tragedy.

Some scholars believe that watching violence on TV relieves a personal need to be violent, others believe that watching TV violence inures and desensitizes us to real violence. Even though I tend to agree with the latter, I make the argument throughout the book that through vicarious experience, one can rid oneself of some of the frustrations we meet daily in a difficult world. I believe this to be true. Still, it is difficult to support an activity whose members seem to have a penchant for violence toward women. I think it's time that the players begin to monitor their own and their team-mates' behavior and leave the tough stuff on the field.

The best football is played hard and fair. Unnecessary roughness and brutality really ruin the game. Attempting to cause serious injury to members of the other team is unnecessary and makes the game ugly. Accepting unnecessary brutality as part of the culture of football contributes to the abysmal behavior among the spectators like some of the things that occurred in the 1994 season at LA Raiders games. It is clear that a culture that accepts savageness among its own will surely turn its head from the resultant violence toward its women.

It's time for those who seem to have a problem to take some lessons from Vance Johnson, formerly of the Denver Broncos. Please, get it together so that I can, in good conscience, get on with telling my sisters about your lovely, exciting, exhilarating game and how to watch and appreciate it.

THE FOOTBALL FAN
(A Dittie)

Fanny the fan waves a flag in one hand,
In the other, the hot dog she bought at a stand.
She jumps and she hollers, appears in a dither,
ignoring the mustard that plopped on her sweater.

Fanny watches with pleasure as the men on the field
crash into each other, it's all so surreal.
The ball is advanced ten yards on the play.
The fans and our Fanny shout hip, hip, hooray!

At the end of the play all the men rise but one.
He lies there in pain with a broken leg bone.
He's carried away and then quickly forgotten.
How fickle these fans, how really quite rotten.

But the fans have their fun and Fanny her zeal -
To her this occasion holds much fannish appeal.
It helps solve her aggressions, her anger and fear.
It might work for you, too, we'll tell you how, here!

CHAPTER 1

A CONTEST OF SPORT

Games, games, games, wonderful inventions of humankind. Take for example the ancient game, Kalaha, where the player strategically attempts to empty the goat turds from the cups of his opponent. Actually, that was the way it was played long ago. Our game has little wooden balls. Most game stores these days do not stock goat doings.

Games have been played by women and men since time began, but what keeps people playing is not altogether clear. For children, it is a kind of practice for later becoming a grown up. Like other kinds of little animals who growl and scratch and jump at each other, little humans play pretend people games: house, trucks, fireman, farmer, Power Ranger, doctor. But for adults, playing games may be related to our instinct to compete for and protect our territory.

Or consider this. Humans are and always have been attracted to drama. In every drama, conflict is central to the event. There is the protagonist, the one we care about, and the antagonist, the villain. There is an outcome or a resolution which brings about a catharsis that blows off steam, relieves tension and clears the air. This is certainly descriptive of the novels we read, the plays and movies we watch, and it also describes a contest of sport. A game. In every drama there is also a lesson, or a demonstration about some aspect of what it is to be human. If one is looking, one can find, too, as a participant or a spectator of a game, a little something about living in the world and how people behave.

We do know that there is in our nature as human beings a continuous yearning to learn new things, to do old things better, to test our position and knowledge and strength. Consider rock climbing or race car driving. Some of us like pushing the envelope even farther than others.

Now, approaching the 21st century, we play games for many reasons. For health, fitness, diversion, to relieve stress, to experience the pleasure of our bodies functioning at peak, to compete with others, to test our abilities. But playing ourselves is quite another thing from watching, and ultimately becoming emotionally involved in the playing of others. We call this being a fan.

The games we watch others play usually require someone doing something to a variously shaped ball with a variously shaped stick.

Golf, for example; what an intriguing idea. Using the smallest sports ball, and clubs, people walk (or are driven) some distance whacking at the ball, trying to hit it into a very small cup placed in the ground many yards away. The players who are really good at this have what is known as a gallery following them along, cheering when the whacking is accurate, when the aim is good. The people that form the gallery are there for the pure joy of watching their guy or gal and are not allowed to participate by taking a swing at the ball themselves. This slow-moving event is viewed by millions on TV and is a high stakes game for the participants; the whole purse up to $2 million, the winner receiving $360,000 for one tournament (e.g., Fulton Allem at the NEC World Series of Golf in Akron, Ohio in 1994).

Many of our games are not essentially physical but consist only of out-strategizing or out-thinking an opponent, as in Kalaha mentioned previously, or chess. And there are running, sliding, jumping, diving or rowing something games. As infinite as human imagination and invention are the games for us to play. And games for us to watch.

The culture and society of whole towns can revolve around games: a Friday night or Saturday afternoon high school or college football game; a little league baseball playoff game. In the mid-sixties, my family moved to West Lafayette, Indiana, from San Francisco so that my husband could attend Purdue University. What did people do in West Lafayette in the mid-sixties? Unlike San Francisco which was busy producing flower children, West Lafayette did big-time college football. (And the weather, of course. And I'm sorry, that was about all!) Have you ever seen the arm wrestling championships broadcast from the small Northern California town, Petaluma? Interesting. The Rose Bowl game, together with the accompanying pageantry, is Pasadena's biggest, grandest event. And in Western Pennsylvania, at their local football games, that's where they grow and harvest young, strong, excellent football players.

Some people insist on making a distinction between games and sports. To them, many sports are games but not all games are sports. For our purposes, we will use the terms interchangeably.

The games we'll be talking about will be the BIG games played by big guys. These are the games we perceive as threatening our relationships and our happy homes. These are the games that our men watch. Hour after hour, every weekend, for nearly six months every year, on the TV or at the stadium. These are Football Games!

The Obstacles

You know the saying, "If you can't beat 'em, join 'em?" I'm sure I'll get some argument about this. Especially when it comes to examining professional football with an intent to understand and even enjoy watching it. And rightly so, with stuff like the following appearing in the sports sections of our newspapers daily:

"I actually had to kick the fat S.O.B. playing against me." The title of the article was, 'And Now They Know How It Feels.' "The tough guy L.A. Raiders got all the worst of it Sunday - - as the 49ers beat em up and piled on the points. . . They didn't just beat a team, they left it in shambles."

And another quote, "I grabbed his face mask - - ripped off his helmet and threw it 20 yards." What this article did not mention is that by grabbing a player's face mask, you could break his neck. And then ripping off his helmet! Oh, my!

In one of the books I used to research the game, I found another related quote:

"Mention the name Conrad Dobler to a defensive player in the 1970's, and that player will immediately flinch. Dobler, who played with the St. Louis Cardinals, New Orleans Saints and Buffalo Bills as an offensive guard, had a reputation for the following: biting fingers, punching stomachs, kicking shins, grabbing face masks, and spitting at players."

In the interest of our current pursuit, I will limit this kind of information. We want to attend to the finesse of a wonderful play, the grace of a wonderful run. We will learn to ignore the louts that are a part of the game and focus on how we can enjoy it. Just understand that even the most mild-mannered gentlemen, in order to be competitive in the game of football, must turn up the testosterone, and sometimes this brings out the worst in them.

We will bypass the seeming brutishness, get by it, so to speak, to figure out why and how to become a fan of football.

And They Get Paid For This

So, how and why do grown men become so wrapped up in and enamored of games? Though professional football and other games of this ilk certainly are games, men have made them into businesses as well. In this country, almost anything that is 'business' is valued.

On TV some years ago, there was a feature story about Donald Sterling, the man who owns the Los Angeles Clippers, a pro basketball team. Mr. Sterling was shown sitting courtside, schmoozing with his entourage. Apparently he had purchased the franchise for a song, as they say, around $1,000,000 and now, a few years later, the team was many times more valuable. The Clippers don't win many games; nonetheless, as would a good old house in California, the dollar value of the team appreciates healthily. The newscaster also informed the single gals in the audience that Mr. Sterling with the appreciating basketball team is married. Few other kinds of news stories would include the marital status of the main character. That's what begins to make becoming a fan interesting.

Professional athletes make millions. *The Sporting News* in January of 1989 listed the 1988 salaries of players in the three major professional sports. It was interesting to note the way the money was divvied up that year in the National Football League (NFL). Four players on the LA Raiders received $1,000,000 or more, while no one on the Pittsburgh Steelers made more than $800,000. John Elway, the quarterback for the Denver Broncos, made two times as much as anyone else on his team. The highest paid annual salary for 1988 went to a rookie and included his signing bonus, Aundray Bruce received $1,900,000 for playing for the Atlanta Falcons. That was five years ago. Where is Mr. Bruce now? He's not listed with the Falcons on their 1994 roster. And who's ever even heard of him? (My scouts tell me he is a second-string linebacker with the Los Angeles Raiders, never having lived up to initial expectations.)

The 1994 salaries were staggering! The player salary expenditures for NFL teams ranged from $30,888,000 for the Pittsburgh Steelers to $42,597,000 for the Washington Redskins, the 'Salary Cap' instituted that year notwithstanding. You may have heard about salary caps as related to the mess in professional baseball. What it means is that no team may spend more than an agreed upon amount on salaries; for the NFL, $36.5 million. Needless to say, this means that prudence must be used when striking a deal with a single player because all the other players must be paid, too. All salaries summed may not, then, exceed the salary cap. Some very creative deals have been struck in the NFL since the advent of the salary cap.

The San Francisco Forty-Niners are very successful. Some say the 1994 team was the greatest team of all time. They won the Super Bowl, as most prognosticators said they would at the beginning of the season. *The 1994 Complete Handbook of Pro Football* gives a description of a number of the NFL players. The book lists seven Niners as having 1994 base salaries of more than $1,000,000. Some of these are:

Jerry Rice, the preeminent wide receiver = $3.75 million
Steve Young, the quarterback = $4.025 million
Brent Jones, tight end and receiver = $1.2 million
And John Taylor, yet another receiver = $1.4 million.

One would surmise that the Niners love those receivers, they were certainly paid well.

In 1981, my son's senior year at Santa Barbara High School, Randall Cunningham was a tall, skinny-looking quarterback who led the school's football team to the California Interscholastic Federation (CIF) playoffs. While I remember attending the game, I do not recall the final outcome. When I began my research for this book and came across the 1988 salaries, I about fell off my library chair reading that our small-town hero had received $1,350,000 that year, quarterbacking for the Philadelphia Eagles. (My son, a fledgling lawyer, was a Public Defender for Alameda County at the time, making $36,000 per year!) In 1994, Randall made a base salary of $2.5 million, in spite of leg injuries that kept him from playing for most of two of the last three seasons. What happened to him and the Eagles in the 1994 season is another story.

In 1994, base pay for starting quarterbacks ranged from $800,000 to $4+ million, nearly all received well over $1 million. At the beginning of the season, *Sports Illustrated* said that quarterback Troy Aikman of the Dallas Cowboys was the highest paid of all players, pulling down $6.25 million. Oh well, after one million, who's counting?

So you see, professional games mean big business and big money. The figures quoted are, again, base salaries, so do not include such things as advertising endorsement contracts, so lucrative for big name athletes. In 1989, the biggest surprise of all was that the richest of the rich was good old golfer, Arnold Palmer. Probably today it would be Michael Jordan or Joe Montana. Maybe tennis player, Andre Aggassi. Someone asked me what in the world do these people do with all this money - - who knows?

So, What About Fans?

What are the ingredients that go into cooking up a good fan? What are the psychological factors that paint a fan picture? The local library has nothing about fans. Nothing in the bookstore either. So, though I know I've read learned articles in the past dealing with the hows and whys of "fan" behavior, I seem to be unable to find any recent literature, nor am I able to adequately explain it. While I can't tell you for certain why a fan behaves as s/he does, I can give you some ideas about it. And, I can teach you how to become one, joining the ranks of the millions worldwide who take pleasure in watching children and grown-ups play games.

Obviously, there is a relationship between why people play games and why people watch others play games. Being a fan is a vicarious experience. Voyeurism of sorts. Being a serious supporter of a sports team seems to come quite naturally to the men in our lives. They can easily while away a weekend sitting on the couch, or if they are less passive, jumping up and down around the living room yelling and screaming to encourage their favorite teams.

Some New Age thinkers would tell us that the energy coming from this seemingly separate being shouting in his own living room combines with all the others like him and those immediately present in the stadium to form a huge force all directed at the few persons competing on the field. In pro basketball, where each team consists of five players, the crowd is perceived as having so much influence that it is referred to as the "sixth man."

Sorting it out, making sense of it, is not easy. Simple diversion from our mundane lives - our sports heros certainly give us that. Perhaps what attracts us is the feeling of togetherness with other like enthusiasts who form a kind of extended family.

It is important to understand, too, that it is almost essential that the chosen team meets with some level of success, else the discomfort and frustration for the fan becomes too great and s/he retreats to other teams or other pastimes. In other words, the feeling of elation and power when a good point is scored is a positive reinforcement. When the game is won, a great, albeit short-lived, sense of joy is experienced by the fan. When this feeling is absent or infrequent, the fan, as we explained, tends to look elsewhere for these good feelings. The whole experience of being a fan involves personal choice. No need to stay with a failing team, we have the right to switch whenever we wish.

There are some fans, however, who might be considered the really good ones, who stay with their teams, go out to the stadium, watch Sunday football to experience loss after loss. We're talking about the dead of winter here. Sitting outside in temperatures at times below freezing. The heartbreak of team loyalty. But, after all, loyalty is a value in this culture!

What's In It For You?

Looking further, what's in it for you? You reasonably sane, intelligent women out there who have picked up this book out of curiosity or perhaps looking for an answer to a real or imagined threat to your partnership with your man. There truly may be some features and benefits for you in joining the millions who love watching sports.

What about broadening your experience of the world you live in. Hey, that's a pretty good reason to learn about something new. Or, you might learn to appreciate the accomplishments of fine professional athletes, their strength, grace and prowess. The excitement can be breathtaking.

You can receive the benefits of vicariously venting hostility. For example, you might be angry at your husband. The game begins. You watch your team out-maneuver and out-power its opponents, you yell and clap and say mean things about the other team. Let it all hang out. It's allowed. As a result, you feel a little better about your husband and treat him a little nicer at dinner.

As I mentioned previously, there is a sense of extended family about belonging to a fan group. People generally support the home team, so there is a kind of ownership connected with the city where you live. It is definitely a group experience and it is fun to belong.

Another benefit of supporting a team is the pure diversion of it. Almost nothing about the game resembles the challenges you face in your regular life. You can completely remove yourself from your daily milieu and lose yourself in a kind of fantasy world where people you don't know become your heros. You can carry your fantasies to the limit, expanding your experience and savoring the moment.

Do you ever catch MTV, the music video station? If not, you probably don't have teenagers living at your house. One Sunday, my daughter and I watched Jon Bon Jovi do his thing. Both of us were adrool as this lovely, sexy young man performed. It was pure pleasure, fantasy, enjoyment, removal, divertissement. And it's really okay.

You know about groupies. Those young women who chase after musicians, adoringly grabbing at their persons in near assaults. Sports fans generally do not carry their enthusiasm to these extremes, but a parallel can certainly be drawn. Your groupie-like attention to certain professional athletes can bring your interest right into the game. We will discuss this aspect of being a fan later.

Fans can be cruel. You need to know that. The great pitching ace Oral Hershiser once said that because he had achieved success, and because he makes so much money, a certain level of performance is expected of him. The people who adored him one day will be the same who boo and pan him on the next if he does not live up to their expectations.

Most fans are indeed fickle. Part of the point of being a fan would be lost if this were not true. If your guy or group of guys is successful, you become successful. If they are not, you are not, because you have thrown your support behind an unsuccessful team. You were unable to rightly select a winner. The world loves a winner. There is power in being a winner or selecting and associating with a winner. There is certainly a dehumanizing aspect to the attitude fans have toward players.

On the other hand, we can hardly walk in their moccasins. They are generally remote. All we know about them is what we're allowed to know. As far as we knew, for example, O.J. Simpson was a talented, gracious, good-hearted hero. Now he's on trial for murder. Whether or not he's found guilty, the general public has glimpsed more of his private life than we ever wanted to know. Such an intimate view is rarely available to fans. It is all a stage, and the players, actors. As fans, we rarely take to heart the real pain of failure felt by a defeated professional athlete. Of course, as a fan, you have the option not to be cruel, but it does seem to be part of what happens.

So. Let's see. Benefits. An activity shared with husband, lover, friends. The big game can be gangs of fun. Super Bowl Sunday is now one of the biggest media events of the year. Millions participate in festivities surrounding the event. You don't want to be left out - people serve yummy noshes at Super Bowl parties. The munchies notwithstanding, it is much more fun if you understand the game.

Attending the big college football games in the fall, in person, is a long-standing American tradition. You should experience this at least once. The leaves turning color, a cool nip to the air. The anticipation of the students filling the stands dressed in their warm, colorful sweaters. The huge marching band with it's marvelous music and well-practiced, well-coifed half-time show. The cute young cheerleaders generating excitement with cart wheels, flips and high-in-the-air pyramid hand stands. It's wonderful. Sort of pure and wholesome. Again, much more fun if you understand the game that they have all come to be a part of.

Football games will not replace the chamber music or the local little theater that you so love. Those will still be a part of your life and will keep you cultured. But you should consider becoming a fan of football. Just for the fun of it!

The intent of this book, then, is to help you understand what it means to be a fan, understand the fundamentals of the game of football, and to help you see how you yourself can become a fan. The how-to of fanaticism. (Yes, it's true, the word fan is a derivative of fanatic.)

You have options. You may read the book from cover to cover. Or, you may chose to read only the chapters that interest you. If things become too technical like in Chapters 4 or 5, or too boring, skip along to something else. But, remember, the more you learn and understand, the more fun you'll have!

CHAPTER 2

BECOMING A FAN

December 31, 1994. Joe Montana, Marcus Allen, Coach Marty Schottenheimer and the Kansas City Chiefs played today. This was the first of a series of play-off games leading to the Super Bowl to be played late in January. Joe Montana, Marcus Allen and the KC Chiefs lost to the Miami Dolphins. It was an excellent game. There were few penalties, one pass interception and one other turnover. Nonetheless, KC was on the losing end of a 27 to 17 score and that was really too bad.

Joe Montana at 38 is a young man - an old man, though, for football. Marcus Allen is 34, also a young man, but for a running back he, too, is getting old. Why should I care? How did I become interested in these two gentlemen and their professional football careers?

Joe Montana was the king in San Francisco for several years. He was the Grand Pooh Bah, and many came to watch the games really to watch him (and Jerry Rice, of course.) He is nice, too; he is smart, he is clever and capable and altogether a class act.

Nonetheless, he was sent on out to Kansas City this year. And the interest I had as a California gal in the exquisite San Francisco quarterback followed him right back there. Now, at 38, people question whether Joe Montana will see another year as a pro football player. He's certainly had his share of injuries over the years, missing at least two games of the 1994 season. But today he was perfect; he could have been 28 rather than 38. No one wants to see him go, but no one wants to see him hurt anymore, either. My guess is, inasmuch as KC lost today and since they did not take it quite as far as Joe would have liked and since he apparently ends the season in good health, he will be back! (Wrong again. In a much ballyhooed, much publicized, much attended celebration, Joe Montana retired from professional football on April 18, 1995.)

Then there's Marcus Allen. How did I come to be interested in him? In one or more of Shakti Gawain's books about meditation and spiritual awakening, Marcus is acknowledged as an inspiration. See, I'm also interested in matters of the spirit. And he is very attractive looking. Furthermore, Marcus is a California guy. He spent his college days at USC, the school my brother attended. Later he signed with the LA Raiders, a disaster for his career. Rumor has it that the owner of the team, Al Davis, put the kibosh on his play time as well as his ball-carrying time so that during what should have been his most productive years, he was robbed of opportunity. Then, at 34, he was turned loose with Joe Montana and the KC Chiefs to have a very special, very successful year.

This is how being a fan works. Though we only know the public side of these big celebrities, we still become attached and interested. We hurt if we imagine that our star may hurt, we are elated and happy if our chosen players meet with success. It helps, being women, if the guys have attributes like intelligence, humor and good looks that make men attractive to us.

The KC - Miami game was an altogether excellent playoff game, though I felt there was at least one bad call from the officials. I thought that Marcus was down before the ball was stripped from him, which caused a turnover, giving the ball to the Dolphins mid-fourth quarter. Our beginning psychology classes tell us that perceptions get altered depending on what we wish to see. Nonetheless, the game was fun and very exciting to watch because people I cared about were playing. That's what it's about, this is being a Fan.

My Indoctrination

I have been a fan for as long as I can remember. My older brother was an athlete and a football player. Though I, too, would have preferred to play on the school team, being a girl, I was relegated to the sidelines and cheerleading. In my small Southern California home town, as in many small suburban and rural towns, the most exciting thing that ever happened was and may still be, the local sports events. The Friday night high school football game during the fall is such an event. Townspeople drive for miles to see their sons and their sons' friends play. A bonfire pep rally is held the night before the BIG GAME, getting everyone in the mood, into a high energy state to WIN! The guys who play are on top of the world. The 'jocks' own the school.

Sometimes, during these early fanwomanship years, a girl learns what the game is about, but more often, she doesn't actually understand much about what the players on the field are doing. The important thing, to her, is to cheer when the cheerleaders tell her to, to laugh and have fun with her friends, to notice and be noticed and to watch for the guy she has her eyes on. And that is

the key and the direction we will take - - the way into fanwomanship. The key is the part about watching for some special guy or
guys.

A young girl with an older brother learns about the game.
Besides, I was a player, too, and could throw a very nice spiral
pass, holding the ball just so with my fingers correctly placed
across the stitches. But I was only allowed to play informally, on
Saturday afternoons, in the vacant lot next to our house. A young
girl who is interested enough can ask and learn. But the best and
easiest way to learn to understand a particular sport is to
participate in it. To play. And young girls have traditionally been
banned from the football field.

Another way women grow up learning about sports is by
having a young man friend who is involved in the sport and in her
and who is willing to share his knowledge with her. I had several
such relationships, not all at once, of course, more or less in
sequence. At a young age I married a man who was a Physical
Education major in college and who later became a football coach.
It was too much fun sitting in the grandstands with other student
wives, many of them chatting about babies and school and clothes
and not having a clue about what their player husbands were
doing on the field. Which shows that, without a certain amount of
directed interest and intent, even women closely associated with
the sport may not get it.

Then I had sons and they played and they became fans as did
my daughter, and on it went. We were a family that loved the
excitement of football and the fun of being fans. And once again,
though it is in some ways brutish, football can be an excellent
outlet for young people. Much better - - controlled violence on the
football field than the gang violence that is ending young lives in
our streets.

Beginning Lessons

The key to enjoying the game is to become involved and to become attached.

In 1968, my six year old son became enamored of Joe Namath, whose football career was much more successful than his movie career. We heard one hot summer day that Joe had come to our small southern California town to shoot a film. My good-natured husband, my older son, my six-year-old and I jumped into the car to track down Mr. Namath for an in-person look and with any luck, an autograph. We spent the better part of two hours attempting to trace the footsteps of the remarkable gentleman, and at last we were successful. On a one-by-two inch scrap of paper, Joe Namath's autograph still decorates my grown-up son's home.

Joe Namath deserved this kind of adoration. With verve, courage, and style, he brought the fledgling American Football League nose to nose with the ancient giant, the National Football League, and led his team to a victorious confrontation. Did he have an arm! Translated: he could really throw a football. And he had a quite a reputation to boot. He was the darling of New York City and a very eligible bachelor for a long time. None of which mattered to my son; he loved Joe Namath because he could play.

Then an interesting thing happened. My young son's admiration for Joe Namath generalized to the Jet's team, then to other New York teams for every other major professional sport. To this day, about 25 years later, he rants and raves about the Knicks and the Mets as well as the Jets. His love continues even though he's never been to New York, and living in California, only rarely gets to see his favorite teams play. What's wrong with the Forty-Niners? And what about the Raiders? These are questions a reasonable person might ask. But, alas, no explanation is forthcoming. The mystery of fan behavior. How does one decide which team to support?

The National Football League (NFL) Teams

Divided into two conferences

National Football Conference   **American Football Conference**

Divided into three divisions

Western Division   **Western Division**

St. Louis Rams   San Diego Chargers
Atlanta Falcons   Los Angeles Raiders
San Francisco Forty-Niners   Seattle Seahawks
New Orleans Saints   Denver Broncos
Carolina Panthers*   Kansas City Chiefs

Central Division   **Central Division**

Green Bay Packers   Houston Oilers
Minnesota Vikings   Cleveland Browns
Chicago Bears   Cincinnati Bengals
Detroit Lions   Pittsburgh Steelers
Tampa Bay Buccaneers   Jacksonville Jaguar*

Eastern Division   **Eastern Division**

Philadelphia Eagles   Miami Dolphins
New York Giants   New York Jets
Washington Redskins   New England Patriots
Arizona Cardinals   Indianapolis Colts
Dallas Cowboys   Buffalo Bills

*New teams in 1995

Appointing Your Team

The most reasonable place to take your first step into the wide world of being a fan, is with a local team. I understand that for some people, the closest city sporting a professional football team may be many miles away. Nonetheless, you may pick the closest.

Or there may be something about a name that intrigues you. For example, astrologically speaking, you may be an Aries, born in late March or early April, so naturally, you would be partial to the St. Louis Rams. Or you may be in love with dolphins, as so many people are these days, so of course you'd pick Miami as your team.

Or you might like to go with a proven winner. Your pick would be the Niners or the Dallas Cowboys!

You can find out who won the whole thing last year and take up with that team. Or you may prefer underdogs, so find out who had the worst win/loss record last year and adopt that team as your own. Or you may pick a team because you liked some player from that team whom you saw interviewed on late night TV or because you saw his wife and liked her. Fans sometimes choose teams because of the coach rather than because of any particular player. My husband lived in Pittsburgh for several years so I am naturally kind of a Pittsburgh fan. I really like their coach, Bill Cowher, voted Coach of the Year in 1992. He seems fair and smart and altogether likable, not taking himself too seriously.

Teams may also become the one you like least because of some player or because of the coach. For example, Buddy Ryan, head coach of the Arizona Cardinals, is to me a particularly unlikable and unattractive human. I will likely never be a fan of that team. And another coach whose name I cannot recall was forever chewing and spitting tobacco for the camera to record. I really loathed that team, too. Having a team that you especially don't like ups the pitch in your involvement in the game. Then, even if your team is not playing, you can enjoy rooting for the team that is playing against the one you really don't like. Some people don't like the Niners simply because they so often win.

You might ask your husband or significant other what team he roots for and select that team for yourself. Or you may ask your man friend who his team's biggest rival is and commence to root for that team. (Comes the demonic laughter! Men usually find this very offensive inasmuch as they have so much emotional investment in their own favorite teams. So this of course is, basically, mean.)

As you can see, the methods of selecting your team are endless. Frankly, there is no rhyme nor reason to how people become fans of a particular team. Some mysterious attraction simply compels them. Something like the manner in which we select our mates.

So, make a decision about what team it will be - - you can change that decision tomorrow, or next week, or next year. The next thing to do is to go to the library and look up all you can about your team. Who owns it, who plays on it, who the stars are, its record last season and so on. *Sports Illustrated* and *Sports Weekly* are good sources for this kind of information. You can write to your team, usually in care of the stadium where it plays, and ask to purchase the yearbook, or some other publication which describes its personnel. **Getting to know about the individuals who make up your new team is more important than understanding what they are doing on the field.**

Who Are The Players On Your Team?

Look at pictures of the young men on your now chosen team. Yes, I know, they are very young, 21 to 40. Occasionally a player plays until he's in his mid to late 40s but that's rare. Generally the players are between the ages of 25 and 35.

Running backs and defensive backs, along with quarterbacks, are generally the best looking gentlemen on the team because they look more human than barnlike. Consider the good looks of Troy Aikman, the quarterback for the Dallas Cowboys, and what about Joe Montana or the long since retired beautiful running back for Chicago, Walter Payton. Marcus Allen, whom we've mentioned before, is also a good looker. Running backs, however, generally have a short life span in pro football, because running as it is done in the NFL is not conducive to healthy knees and legs.

People's tastes vary, though, and you may find that the houses who play on the front line, (see Chapter 3) or linebackers, like Kevin Green of the Pittsburgh Steelers, are more your cup of tea. It's true, they're not all that bad, actually - they're quite manly, and they will probably be around longer for you to admire. The point is to find one or two or three players that you find attractive. Hide a picture of the one or ones you like best in your wallet. Find out who these guys are. Learn about where they grew up, how many brothers and sisters they had, if they're married, and for how long, and how many children they have. Music groupies learn everything about the musicians in their favorite bands, sports groupies learn everything about the players on their favorite team. As I said, there is a significant parallel between groupies and sports fans.

Groupies and Fannies

While there are all kinds of fans and all kinds of groupies, they have certain things in common. Five years ago, the world mourned the death of Lucille Ball. No one suspected that her loss would be so widely and generally felt. One gentlemen told a TV interviewer that he was the BEST and BIGGEST fan, that his bedroom was wallpapered with different Lucy photos. The TV camera scanned all those photos for the viewers to see. Unbelievable. I suspect that all that collecting gave the man a good deal of pleasure.

Years ago, when my daughter was 12, her room was similarly wallpapered with Michael Jackson pictures. When friends asked me

about her and what she did with her time, I replied that she did
Michael Jackson. She didn't care for reading but she read vora-
ciously everything that was published about Michael.

One day, she and I and one of her friends spent several hours
cruising the hills of Encino, in Southern California, with scant
directions, attempting to locate the Jackson family home. When we
finally found it, we knew we had arrived because there were about
20 people just standing there, on the road, in front of high brick
walls and an equally high iron gate. They could see nothing
beyond those walls.

They seemed to be standing, these fans of Michael Jackson,
keeping vigil over the house just in case someone should leave the
property, or arrive. Hey, I was just the driver! Seemed pretty
strange to me. But my daughter had fun and happily outgrew the
whole obsession in a year or so, much to the relief of her older
brothers who were afraid for her healthy growth and development.
A divertissement, pure and simple, a crush, disappearing with
some maturity. A pastime that gave my daughter harmless
pleasure. It's okay to have okay heros.

I want to be quite clear about this. You should not expect nor
attempt to establish any sort of a reciprocal relationship with any
player. Rather, you want to establish a kind of fantasy situation
where you only expect to admire from afar. No more!

Groupies sometimes tend to become over zealous, coming close
to injuring the very object of their enthusiasm. Remember Beetle
mania? We'll be having none of that. Neither do we want to be so
persistent as to endanger anyone's life. If you read the
newspapers, you know that there have been many incidents
abroad where people have been killed due to their enthusiasm at
soccer games. At one such event, within the last few years, 94
people were killed.

Please! You're in this to have fun, to heighten your knowledge of football and a particular chosen team, and to share with friends and loved ones the fun of being a fan. The FUN. None of us is really interested in fanaticism.

Connecting With Your Team

So, continuing from that departure, you want to learn about some of the players on your team, or the coach, or the owner. Some way to connect your interest to this team. It is made up of people. The people are what make it interesting. Objectively viewed, the game can seem ridiculous; except for the talent and grace in the running or passing, or some of the clever strategizing, the game can appear altogether nonsensical. Women seem to hold that view more than men.

But, guess what. It's not important. What is important is that little Joe Blow from Nebraska is making it big with the Detroit Lions. That's what will keep you interested, that's what is interesting about the game.

As soon as you learn about Joe Blow, you will be watching for him. When he makes a good play you will be pleased, thrilled even. You will feel a definite emotional involvement. It is as if someone you know personally has been successful and is a winner.

All this is enhanced if your team is located in the city or town where you live. Your hometown boy makes good. Your hometown team makes good. Your hero runs so gracefully, or was successful in blocking the opponent, allowing his own team to score, or he sacked the opposing quarterback.

Be sure to ascertain the jersey numbers of your special players so you can find them, and **as you watch for them, you will begin to put together what they are doing and what is actually happening on the field**. This book will assist in that, as will other books on football you can find in your library or bookstore. But the real trick to becoming a fan is having a hero or heros whom you can talk about as though you were talking about a beloved, admired friend, lover, or relative.

You can see that, for women, fannishness has to do most with the players who make up the team. **It is, therefore, a game of people (not of inches, as you may have heard.)**

The Sports Page

You can enhance your lessons in fanwomanship by reading the sports page in the newspaper. It often resembles a gossip column in the reportage of the activities, events, and play of the game, and even more, in the stories about the public/personal lives of the people. It's kind of amusing because while women are supposed to be so enthralled with gossip, the man's world of sports and its media is a very gossipy kind of environment. The slightest hint of a scandal is followed daily in the media - - Darryl Strawberry (a base-ball player) for example, and his drug wars.

Generally, the scandals usually take one of three paths: drugs, gambling, or spousal abuse. Pretty serious, for sure, but you don't have to continue being a fan of someone whose morals you don't approve or who does things you don't like. These are humans, too; often very young humans with too much money. Pick someone else!

You can see that you can research your team as you would any other subject that interests you, read your newspaper's sports section, read sports magazines and watch the evening sports news on TV. You'll become knowledgeable, have fun, and enhance your 'fanability'. **Ownership and connection are the keys to becoming a fan. Belonging to a team that belongs to you.**

CHAPTER 3

THE PROLATE SPHEROID

I picked up an encyclopedia to see how football was explained. I thought what I read there was interesting, but would probably be confusing and baffling to the new student.

"Outdoor game, played by two opposing teams with a ball of various types, usually an *inflated bladder* in a leather or rubber cover, spherical or *ellipsoidal* in shape."

And.

"American football is played by two teams, each made up of 11 players, with a ball consisting of an inflated rubber bladder encased in a leather or rubber cover. The ball is a *prolate spheroid*, having a circumference of 28 - 28 1/2 inches about the long axis and 21 1/4 - 21 1/2 inches about the short axis; it weighs between 14 and 15 ounces."

The italics are mine. If, in fact, you really don't know what a football looks or feels like, you may want to take a trip to your nearest sporting goods store and hold one. Traditionally, these balls are called "pigskins", though in fact they are no longer made of pig parts, but rather are usually constructed of bumpy leather.

At this point it's interesting to note the difference between what we in this country and what most people around the world call football. In the summer of 1994, The World Cup Soccer tournament was held in the United States. If you watched any of those wonderfully exciting games, you would know that that game is played with a round ball with black and white pentagonal patches. Quite different from our prolate spheroid, and a different game altogether. But - called football in many other places. Rugby, a similar game to American football, is called football too, in some necks of some woods. (In soccer, they call the playing field a pitch. I so love that part.)

So, according to our encyclopedia, we have a Prolate Spheroid, (a ball), and 11 people on each team. A single game is comprised of only two opposing teams. That is, there are not several other teams waiting on the sidelines to play. One team plays a different team each week during the season until each team has played each other team in their group of teams (league/division) at least once.

The season for professional football runs from late August when preseason games are played, to late in January, ending with the Super Bowl.

Game Running Time

Each game consists of one hour of playing time (Fig. 3.1). The hour is broken up into four quarters. At the end of the first and third quarters, there is a 2-minute break while the teams trade places on the field so they switch directions. At half-time, there is a 12-minute break during which the teams leave the field. While the

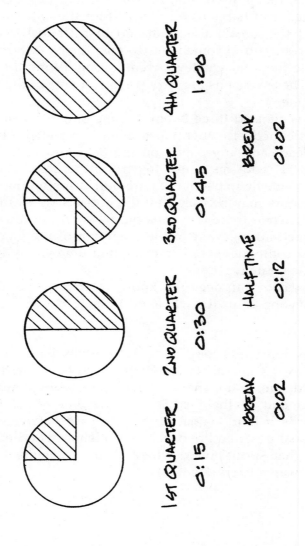

THE CLOCK

1ST QUARTER	2ND QUARTER	3RD QUARTER	4th QUARTER
0:15	0:30	0:45	1:00
BREAK	HALFTIME	BREAK	
0:02	0:12	0:02	

ELAPSED TIME: 3 HOURS

FIG. 3:1

teams are gone, marching bands, majorettes, and flag twirlers per-
form, and other stuff happens on the field for the entertainment of
the crowd. At this break, the teams go to their locker rooms to
strategize, to rest, and in some cases to give their coach the opportunity to berate them for whatever went wrong during the first half
of the game. These sessions are very private, a part of the game we
can only imagine.

Each team is allowed three 2-minute time-outs per half. When a
play ("play" defined elsewhere) has been completed, the ball is
considered "dead" and any player on the field may call a time-out
by signaling a "T" with his hands toward any official. That official
then blows his whistle to begin the time-out, stopping the clock.

Other time-outs may be called by the officials when there is an
injured player, when there is a penalty, or when the officials need
to discuss something relevant to the operation of the game. Time-
outs and other components of game running time are an important
aspect of game strategy.

For now, what you need to know is that while the game
running time is one hour, the whole event takes closer to three.

The Field

The field is 120 yards long and 53 1/3 yards wide. The actual
playing area is 100 yards long. Each 5 yards is marked from
sideline to sideline, with shorter hash marks designating every
yard. At each end of the field is the goal line. Goal posts are
located 10 yards behind a goal line. The space between the goal
line and the goal posts and between the sidelines is called the end
zone. This is that special place where all the excitement happens
and everyone wants to go (Fig. 3:2).

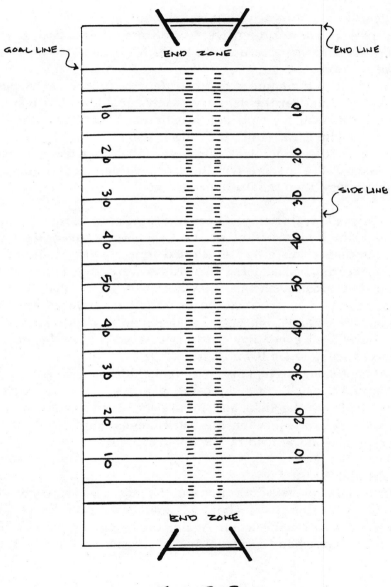

FIG. 3:2

The People

All players are not offensive, as you may think. Each team has an *offensive* and *defensive* unit. Each team also has what are called the *special teams*.

The point of the game is for the offensive unit to carry, pass, or kick the football over the defensive team's goal line. The way this is accomplished will be explained in Chapter 5 entitled "Blue 46. . . Blue 46. . .Hut Hut, Hut!" It is the mission of the defensive unit not to allow the opponents' offensive unit to get the ball over its goal line because a score will then be awarded to the opponents. The defenders, then, guard their own goal.

Four Downs/Plays/Attempts/Tries to Progress 10 Yards

The team in possession of the ball at any given time is the offensive team. This group is allotted four downs (attempts/plays) to advance the ball at least 10 yards toward the defenders' goal line. If they accomplish this, they are awarded another set of four downs in which to advance the ball another 10 yards, and so on until a score is made. Since, as I said, single yards are marked with hash marks and every five yards is marked across the field, you can easily see how far 10 yards is.

If the offensive unit fails to advance 10 yards in four tries, it must forfeit the ball to the opposing team, which asks its defensive fellows to leave the field and invites its offensive bunch to now participate. Likewise, when the ball changes hands, the offense is now replaced on the field by the defensive guys.

The People, Again

Forty-eight players suit up and 53 are listed on the roster, though each team pays about 60 members. Each player has a designated role on the team. Again, the offensive players are the ones who play when their team has possession of the ball; they are trying to advance the ball to the goal line. The defensive players are those who are trying not to allow this advancement by the other team. In case you hadn't noticed, the terms <u>offense, offensive unit, offensive team</u> and <u>offensive guys</u> refer to the same group.

And there are one or two more types of players who make up what are known as <u>special teams</u>. These play only in interim situations such as during kick offs and when a punt is expected. We will explain these events and more about the players later.

There are, at any given time, other folks on the field of play, wearing white knickerbockers, black and white striped shirts and funny little hats, well, baseball hats these days. These guys are the <u>Officials</u>. Sounds important, doesn't it? There are seven officials for each game. There used to be one more in a booth checking out video tapes of plays to ascertain whether a misapplication of the rules had occurred. The NFL subsequently did away with this one.

The Seven Officials (Fig. 3:3)

<u>Referee</u>: The chief official. He settles disputes among the officials and stands behind the offensive backfield.

<u>Umpire</u>: Is concerned with the number of players at the line of scrimmage (explained later). This official is also interested in the players' equipment and inspects it before the game.

<u>Linesman</u>: Watches for problems at the beginning of each play. He also interfaces with the officials on the sideline who keep track of downs and carry the 10 yard chain markers.

<u>Line Judge</u>: Keeps track of the time, especially if the game clock quits working.

<u>Back Judge</u>: Keeps track of action in the defensive backfield.

<u>Side Judge</u>: Also keeps track of the action in the defensive backfield, but on the other side of the field.

<u>Field Judge</u>: Covers the punt returns and long passes, so stands behind the defensive backfield.

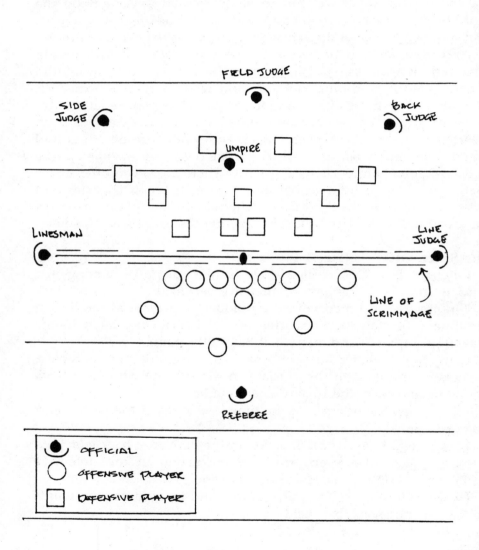

FIELD JUDGE

SIDE JUDGE

BACK JUDGE

UMPIRE

LINESMAN

LINE JUDGE

LINE OF SCRIMMAGE

REFEREE

OFFICIAL
OFFENSIVE PLAYER
DEFENSIVE PLAYER

FIG. 3:3

There are also six <u>assistant officials</u> positioned along the sideline keeping track of downs, yardage, ball position and so on. You can spot these assistants by their day-glo attire, designed to keep the players from bumping into them. There is also, hidden somewhere near the field or in the stands, the official time keeper; where or who this person is may never be known.

In every large stadium, there is a large visible clock that is operated by the invisible time keeper. The clock makes it possible for everyone to know how much time remains in the game, which is a very important something to know. In general, the officials keep track of the time and the rules of the game. Sometimes intentionally and sometimes unintentionally, players break the rules, and there are many to break. The officials mete out appropriate penalties for rule infractions. The officials are charged with keeping the game and the frequent flaring tempers under control.

We will further discuss the officials' duties and list the most common rules elsewhere, but suffice it to say that these fellows in the striped shirts have a right to be there and are fairly important to the conduct of the game. (The encyclopedia says, "Play is supervised by *im*partial officials." Well, wouldn't you hope they were impartial else their function would be rather pointless!)

And there are the coaches and other staff members whose charge it is to direct the functioning of the team. Coaches are important in the game, bigwigs, you might say. A very interesting bunch. It's clear that to be the coach of a high-powered, big-money professional sports team, a man would have to have nerves of steal. Ice water in his veins. (An aside: there are no women coaches, no female players; this is a man's world, this pro football.) The job of coach is to teach, to inspire, to cajole, to, in general, run the team. A big job, lots of responsibility, and of course, big pay.

The coaches and coaching staff can be seen pacing on the sidelines between the 35-yard lines, in the midst of the team players who are not at this moment engaged in the game. Each coach and his assistants dress and outfit themselves uniquely from all other coaches. Most wear earphones, allowing them to converse with other coaches, whose position high above the field affords them a better view of the overall proceedings. Some coaches carry a clipboard. Some dress very casually; tennis shoes, khakis and sweater. Others may wear a team warm-up suit and still others will be dressed to the nines in expensive three-piece suits. Some wear cowboy hats, others wear baseball caps. Some look as though they had just stepped out of *Gentleman's Quarterly.* (Frankly, all things considered, I think the basketball coaches are a better looking, better dressed bunch. Take Pat Reilly, for example.)

There are still more people associated with the ball game. The cheerleaders have a function - - exactly what it is is not clear, well, really, it is to entertain. They assist in generating the kind of group energy and force we talked about in Chapter One. I was a cheerleader in high school. We wore heavy sweaters and pleated skirts to our knees. We had not one provocative routine in our repertoire - - - boooorrrring. Frankly, I don't know how it is now, but in high school, few of the cheerleaders knew much about the game and most were hard pressed to decide what sort of inspir- ation was called for at any given time. "Hold that line! Hold that line!" or "Hey, hey, (clap clap) ho, ho, (clap, clap). Let's get that ball and really go!" Oh, well. Safe to say that the professional cheer-leaders don't have to know much about the game either. They just have to know how to dance.

There are also the announcers. Announcers at the stadium don't describe the game play for play but introduce players, activities, and so on. The broadcasting announcers, on the other hand, account for the action exactly as it unfolds. Good announcers enhance interest by telling gossipy little things about individual players and by explaining the finer nuances of the game. Good announcers make the game easier to follow, understand, and enjoy.

So, those are the people who set the stage and provide the action at the football game. All that is missing is the fan. Having fans being fans is essential to the successful functioning of a ball team. And it must not go unnoted that at least part of the big money associated with the game comes from the fans.

Scoring

Obviously, the object of the game is for each team to score more points than its opponent. There are five ways to score points. These are:

1. **Touchdown (TD)** = 6 points
2. **Conversion**, point(s) after touchdown = 1 or 2 points
3. **Field Goal** = 3 points
4. **Safety** = 2 points
5. If a team forfeits, the score is 1 - 0.

A **touchdown** means that by virtue of one of several possible strategies, the ball has been propelled across the goal line. By "propelled", we mean either thrown and caught, or carried. It's not to the advantage of the offense to attempt to roll or bounce the ball to one another across the goal line. These strange shaped footballs, prolate spheroids, bounce erratically, as one might expect a prolate spheroid to do. Besides, this is not basketball and this activity is against the rules. Someone must be handed the ball and run with it over the goal line, or someone must throw the ball to someone in the end zone, or someone must throw the ball to someone who then runs into the end zone. Touchdown! Six points!

A team can also score a TD if a player falls on a loose ball behind their opponents' goal line, this only if the ball is in play.

After a touchdown occurs, the successful team is awarded an attempt to score even more points; this is called a **conversion** or **point (s) after touchdown**. (There is also another event known as a conversion but we're trying to abide by the rule of keeping this simple.) Maybe this event is called a conversion because the team has the opportunity to convert its score from 6 to 7 or 8.

So, there are two ways to convert. One is by a place kick between the goal posts over the cross bar (Fig 4:1). This kick play begins at the 2-yard line, is centered (more on centering later) to a holder who holds it just so (with the stitches away from the kicker) on the ground at the 9-yard line. Then the kicker steps up and kicks it, hopefully through the goal posts. Since the kicker kicks from the 9, that makes it about a 19-yard kick including the additional 10 yards for the end zone. This is the **One Point Conversion**. The **Two Point Conversion** is a running or pass play similar to the one that gained the score in the first place.

The opportunity to convert is not uncontested. These plays are the same as any other plays in the game, with the defense attempting to keep the offense from doing what it wants to do.

When a team is on its last try to gain 10 yards (fourth down) or if time is running out in the half or in the game, and if the team is within at least 35 yards of the opposing goal line, a **Field Goal** might be attempted. Thirty-five yards, because any farther back would be too far for the kicker to kick the ball. It's the offensive team's choice. The field goal is similar to the one point conversion. To conduct a field goal, the ball is snapped from the center to the holder guy who places the ball on the ground about seven yards behind the line where the play began (Fig. 4:1 Note: the line of scrimmage is at the 2-yard line for conversions, but changes with each FG play). The kicker steps up and kicks the ball through the goal posts and over the cross bar. Yay! Three points!

And the last way to acquire points is a **Safety**. If the offense is caught with the ball behind its own goal line, a safety is scored by the defensive team. Two points! (This is not to be confused with a **touchback** where the team receiving a kick downs the ball behind its own goal line, causing the play to end.)

The Game Begins - Offensive Team

Before the game begins, one of the officials tosses a coin to determine which team will kick off, which will receive and which goal each team will defend. At a kick off, the kicking team lines up at or behind it's 30-yard line. One of the team members kicks the ball off a gismo called a tee toward the opposing team (Fig. 4:3). At this time, the special teams are on the field, since the kick off is a special occasion. The kicker is well paid for his talent of being able to place kick the ball appropriately at the other team.

Now, the team that receives the ball is the offensive team, as described above, and the kicking team becomes the defensive team. It's exciting to see a member of the offensive special team receive the ball and run all the way back across the defending special team's goal line. but don't hold your breath. Usually, someone catches the kicked ball and runs only a few yards forward before the defense piles on him and stops his forward motion, summarily ending that play.

At this point, a lot of commotion takes place while players are leaving the field, being replaced by others now getting ready to come on.

The members of the offensive team, now in possession of the ball, get into a circle and lean over. This is called a huddle. The odd configuration of the huddle begins each play and allows the quarterback (QB), the sort of on-field leader of the team, to give orders about the strategy which will immediately be employed to move the ball forward toward the opponent's goal line. By now the

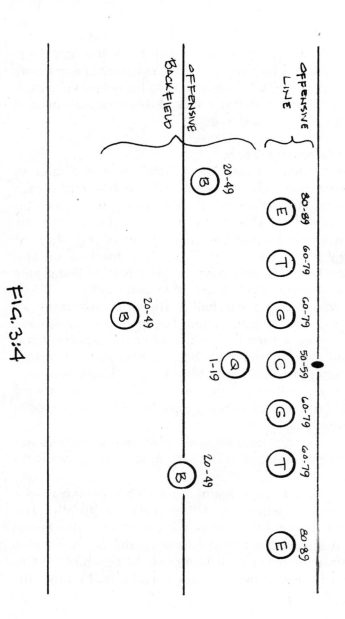

FIG. 3:4

THE OFFENSIVE CONFIGURATION

ball probably rests around the offensive team's 20-yard line.

Orders having been given, the offense streams out from the huddle to a prearranged formation on the field.

The offense must have at least seven people in a line parallel to the ball (the front line). The four other team members stand behind in a sort of second tier (the backfield). (Fig. 3:4) The players on the front line are called offensive linemen and consist of one center, two guards, two tackles, and two ends. The ends are called, relative to their position on the line, split end or tight end. (Most of the players do have pretty tight little ends!)

The people in the backfield are the QB, and two people who used to be called halfbacks but are now called many things depending on where they are told to stand. They may be called setback, tailbacks, or slotbacks. One is usually called a flanker back or wide receiver. And the last player has been commonly called a fullback, but, this player, too, may be known as setback, running back or any of the rest of the possible names.

So, the back field consists of the QB and three running backs with various talents. As we said, one is a wide receiver. Usually one will be a fleet-footed, fast-running ball carrier. Another will also be a ball carrier, but may also be a good blocker or even a pass receiver. Often, one is a burly, sturdy runner who is very strong, as fullbacks used to be, and can be counted on to gain short yardage through muscle and stamina alone.

Each player has a different role. You will notice that the people in the center of the front line are the biggest on the field. It's their job to knock down, without jabbing or holding, everyone who isn't wearing one of their own color of jerseys. This maneuver is known as blocking and as you can guess, it ain't easy. Try knocking down anything, even an inanimate object, without holding on, much less the moving houses on the football field. And they have to knock down their opponents in a particular direction!

The purpose of the offensive linemen knocking everyone down is to allow their own backfield players to run or pass the ball forward to gain the ten yards for a first down, or even better, to advance the ball to the goal line for a score. The purpose of the defensive line knocking people down is to get to whomever has the ball at that moment and stop the play. You can tell who the linemen known as guards and tackles are because the numbers on their jerseys range from 60 to 79.

The center player on the front line has the job of handing, "centering", "hiking", or "snapping" the ball to the QB to begin each play. Then he, too, nudges everyone out of the way. The numbers on the centers will be from 50 to 59. Linebackers may have these numbers, too, so keeping track of players' positions by num-ber can be tricky.

The end players on the front line block, too, but they may also be receivers, meaning that the QB may pass them the ball, which they in turn may carry toward the goal line. The ends will be seen in numbers ranging from 80 to 89.

As we said before, the QB directs the action of the team on the field, though the actual strategy is planned by the coach. As the play begins, the QB accepts the ball from behind the center and between the center's legs and executes the prearranged activities, designed to move the ball down field.

To explain this more clearly, the center bends over the ball which is lying on the ground, picks it up, and hands or tosses it backwards between his legs to the QB who, in some cases, is standing intimately close to the center's backside. The center then proceeds to knock everybody on the opposing team down while the QB either hands the ball off to someone else to run with, or passes the ball to an eligible receiver, who catches it and runs on, or keeps the ball and runs with it himself. The numbers on the

QB's back range from 1 to 19 - - (Joe Montana, #19!) The kickers, whom we previously mentioned, also wear this range of numbers.

The setbacks have several roles. They may be handed the ball, in which case they run forward through all the opposing players who have been knocked down by the front line. They may block to protect their QB while he decides what's best to do with the ball as the play unfolds, or they may block someone making way for a running back, or they may block someone, and then run furiously down field to receive a pass from the QB. The numbers on these backfield folks range from 20 to 49.

So, there are the offensive players and their roles.

The Defensive Team

In the meantime, while the offensive team huddles and prepares to baffle the defenders with some ingenious play or another, the defense sets up to render the offense impotent. Further, it is the job of the defense to get that ball away from the offense and return it to its own team so it may attempt to score.

The positions and roles of the defensive team seem more complicated than those for the offense. There is no regulation about how many people must be where, except that they must stand behind, they may not encroach onto or over the plane of where the ball sits on the field - - the <u>line of scrimmage</u>, the <u>scrimmage line</u>. More about this invisible line later. Early on, team members played both defense and offense, so the names of the players for either activity were the same. Now that there are specialized teams, the names of the positions have varied to some extent. One can generally think of the defense as having a center, guards, tackles, ends and so on; that may make it easier (Fig. 3:5).

But, in fact, it has become more complicated. It is common to have only four players on the front line of the defense. These

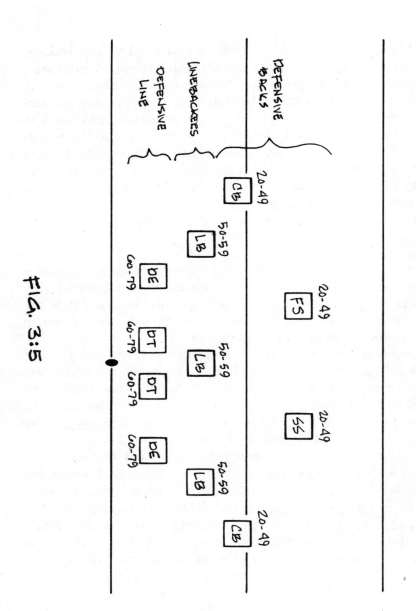

FIG. 3:5

THE DEFENSIVE CONFIGURATION

would be two tackles and two ends. Or if there are six men in the front, these would be two guards, two tackles, and two ends. In the so-called "nickle" defense, two ends and a nose guard are on the front line. All these players will carry numbers from 60 to 79 on their jersey.

Let's proceed with four men on the defensive front line; then there would be three men in the second tier. These are called linebackers, for obvious reasons. Their numbers range from 50 to 59 and from 90 to 99.

Since we have now used up seven of our defensive players, we know that further back on the field we will see four more players scattered about. The generic name for these guys is defensive back. They may be variously called cornerback, defensive halfback, or safety (not to be confused with the method of scoring two points). You will see the numbers 20 to 49 on their backs. Where exactly all these people are located on the field depends on how they anticipate the offense will behave on the next play.

In other words, if the defense thinks the offensive unit will call a long pass play, more players would hang around in the backfield. If they think the play will be run to the right, they might have more players standing on that side of the field. It is all quite arbitrary. Part of the skill of the defense is to predict what the offense intends to do. To out-guess them so to speak, and to be ready to stop them.

As soon as the ball is centered, the defensive front line rushes in to put a stop to the action right now. Whether to keep the QB from passing or to keep a running play from developing, it is the front line's job to allow no player to advance past the scrimmage line. In fact, if they can stop the play somewhere behind the scrimmage line, forcing the offense to lose ground, they have accomplished something swell.

For example, if the defense tackles the QB, who is attempting to pass the ball before he does so, this is called a "sack" and is cause for celebration. Actually, elaborate celebrations on the field for this occasion have been prohibited, but in the past, the sacker had been known to do various unrehearsed dances and gestures around the sackee, much to the chagrin and irritation of the offensive team, not to mention the sacked one. Too bad they can't do this anymore; it was pretty interesting to watch.

The linebackers back up the front line, much as a reinforcement. If a runner has started, has managed to find an opening, and has advanced past the front line players, it is left for the linebackers to come on in and assist in stopping everything - - well, everyone. Remember that this hole that has been found by the running back is a result of the offensive front line bumping everyone down on the defensive front line in just the right direction so that a hole is created for the runner to run through. Linebackers also defend against short pass plays.

Cornerbacks defend against passes and wide running plays. The safeties defend against long passes, and attempt to take down a runner who has broken through the main body of players to the open field. The safeties are an interesting bunch because they are fleet of foot and may often be seen having a sprinting race with an equally fleet pass receiver or running back.

Besides stopping the offensive play quickly and efficiently, as we said, it is the charge of the defense to regain possession of the ball. This is accomplished in several different ways. One is by keeping the offense from gaining the 10 yards in four downs as we have repeatedly discussed, in which case the ball will be handed over or punted to the defensive (which immediately becomes the offensive) team.

Punted. . . the ball is snapped from the center to the kicker, who, without the assistance of a holder, drops and then kicks the ball before it hits the ground, into the defensive team's end of the field (Fig. 4:2). This kicking is done by the place-kicker especially trained to do so. If the offense is within 35 yards of the defenders' goal line, the offense may attempt a field goal. If the attempt is unsuccessful, the defenders then get the ball where the field goal attempt was made - that is - from the point where it was kicked.

Another way to regain possession is to cause a turnover. One way to cause a turnover is to intercept a pass intended for a member of the other team. An interception may be legally accomplished by any member of the defensive team; but somehow, one expects the defensive backs to do the intercepting. If a defensive lineman comes upon an errant pass and catches it, it is a rare and very special occasion for that player. He may lumber a ways down the field, but usually the faster backfield players will catch up to and tackle him before he scores a touchdown. (The dictionary says, "Tackle: a seizing or grasping." That's close enough.)

If a person carrying the ball is bumped hard enough, or if the ball is slippery from the rain, or if the ball carrier has a propensity for doing so, the ball may be fumbled (dropped) from his hands and any player on the field may retrieve it. When there is a fumble, there is usually a big scramble on the field. Whether or not players recovered the ball, they certainly want the officials to believe they did, so no one gets up out of the pile-on until it is absolutely necessary.

Another way to lose the ball is to muff a punt or fair catch. That is, the kick comes into a special team backfield player's hands and he fails to make the catch. Anyone can scramble to retrieve the ball at that point. However, a muffed ball may not be advanced by the kicking team; rather, the next play begins where the muffed ball was recovered.

(A fair catch is when the kicked ball is coming to the backfield person and he makes a special gesture, puts his hand in the air, so that no one may then tackle or bump him while he is doing the catching. The next play begins where the fair catch took place.)

The Scrimmage

Don't you love it? A new language. The origin? Skirmish, of course. The ball lies on the skirmish line, which before the play begins, is an imaginary strip across the field the width of the football. That is, the scrimmage line, before the play begins, is as wide as the football is long. As soon as the ball is released from the center, the skirmish line becomes just a narrow line. If there were not that wide skirmish band, the teams would bump into each other while they get positioned, waiting for the next play to begin. The skirmish line, is, then, where one play ends and the next play begins. (Figs. 3:3, 3:4, 3:5.)

When the ball is in play, a skirmish/scrimmage is going on. The people who are really involved in this thing call this a scrimmage, so we will too.

In the next chapter, we will look at the general planning of the game, how game decisions are made and what those decisions are based upon. In Chapter 5, I will describe a few simple plays; ways to advance the ball as is the purpose in all this. These are the organized, systematized methods and schemes used by the offense to outsmart the defense. The defensive team has sort-of-plays too, but they are more reactive than proactive, because they are in response to the cleverly devised conducts of the offense.

As I pointed out in Chapter 1, the discussions in Chapters 4 and 5 are interesting but technical, and require energy and concentration. You may not consider them fun. Give them a try, a skim at least, then move on to Chapter 6 and come back to these chapters later when you think you might more enjoy them, maybe after you've seen a couple of games. This is about pleasure, so read the parts you want to, ignore the ones you don't.

CHAPTER 4

STRATEGIC PLANNING

E | ach professional team has a huge organization
    | supporting it. There are the head coach and up to
    | twelve assistant coaches responsible for offense,
defense, kicking, passing, receiving, special teams and on and on.
There are the men and women in the front office who manage the
business affairs of the team, and there are the scouts and personnel
people. As we pointed out earlier, this is big business - if games
are not won, if big TV contracts are not forthcoming, if attendance
is not high, in short, if the team is not successful and profitable for
the owners, heads role. The business aspects are part of the overall
strategy of the game.

Each team has scouts who run around watching films of other
teams and go to other teams' games watching players, team
strategies and key plays of those teams. They are also looking at

different players to recommend to coaches and owners. This, too, is part of the overall strategy of the game.

Strategy, then, does not consist only of what the players are doing on the field at any given time, but rather, how to outsmart the other team by knowing ahead of time how it responds in certain situations and where its weaknesses lie. The overall strategy, the detective work, hiring and firing of personnel, are all geared, naturally enough, toward the important goal of the game: WINNING.

The Team Scheme

Each team has a unique personality which arises from the overall strategy or philosophy of the head coach and owner or owners. It's sometimes difficult to say which has the most influence on an organization, but certainly while the coach designs the activities of the team, the owner must approve of the general design, approve of the coach, allow him to coach and pay him, thereby influencing the outcome even by his/her acquiescence. (Though most owners are hims, the owner of the LA/St. Louis Rams is a her, Georgia Frontiere.)

The best organizations work as teams from top to bottom, including players, coaches, owners, and support people. Players will not play well with people they don't feel have treated them fairly, or whom they really don't like or trust.

Teams can be described by a general theme that typifies its unique personality. For example, a team may be said to have a "run n' shoot" offense. This means that they use four wide receivers (players who catch passes - two split ends and two backs far out to each side) and only one running back. The running back can also be a receiver but may get the ball when the quarterback sees that all of his potential receivers are well covered by defensive players. This general strategy requires a quarterback who thinks well and who can throw fast, that is, release the ball rapidly.

Some teams are known for their defensive expertise, others for their great passing game because they have a very good quarterback, and still other teams prefer a running strategy, usually because of the way the coach views the game. The talent on the squad in any given year will strongly influence its style of play.

Game Plan

Before each game, all the team's coaches meet to construct a game plan. They have a good idea what to expect from the other team because of the scouting reports they have received. The scouts have prepared frequency charts for key players on the opposition, detailing how these players are likely to move. Coaches know the other team's defensive shortcomings and its offensive strengths. They also know those things for their own team. With all this information, the coaches construct a game plan.

The plan may consist of an exact scripting of the first several plays or it may simply be a general response based on the knowledge they have received about the other team. Each player, before the game, is given his individual game plan to memorize that enumerates exactly what is expected of him.

If the opposition has a splendid wide receiver, like Jerry Rice for example, part of the defensive backs' game plan may be to double-team him. That means to have two players defending him, trying to keep him from catching passes.

Game plans may be built around the expertise of one player or all. If a team has an exceptional passing quarterbacl, its offense will be built around that player. Of course, the opposing team has scouted that quarterback and will build its defense around stopping him.

The pitfalls of a rigid game plan are clear. If the key player is hurt, the plan goes into the toilet. If the opposing team pulls some new tricks out of the hat, the defense must adjust; again their original ideas about what should happen are not going to work.

To Run or To Pass, That Is The Question

Some teams prefer to keep the ball on the ground, grinding out yardage through running plays. Other teams may not have the good runner who can be depended on to carry the ball at least 5 yards on any given play, so they rely more on their passing game. The most successful teams have a balance, a nice combination of both running and passing.

There are times when a passing play is needed and times when a team should select a run. For example, if it is third down with long yardage to gain for the first down, a pass play is usually going to be employed. If the offense is on the one-foot line, nearly at the goal line, a running play, maybe a sneak through the middle, will be chosen.

There are times when running or passing plays are called simply to realign the defense so that a more desirable play can be called on the next down.

Surprise is the essential element in all considerations regarding when to choose which play. Often a play will be selected by the coach but when the quarterback sees how the defense has lined up, he changes the call at the line of scrimmage using an "audible" (code words shouted to his players like "46 Blue. . . 46 Blue. . . Hut hut, hut!") signaling a different play than the one designated in the huddle. More about audibles later.

Using Time Strategically

Ball control is a notion that relates to time considerations. Generally, it can be said that the team that has possession of the ball longer during the game has the best chance of ending up with the highest score. A team maintains control of the ball through sustained drives consistently completing yardage for first downs, moving the ball toward the ultimate goal. This takes time.

Especially when close to the end of a game, when the team in possession of the ball is ahead and wants to keep its opponents from catching up, it will employ a careful ball control strategy to use up the time on the clock so that the other team does not get another chance to score.

Actually, the most exciting events surrounding the consideration of time take place during the last two minutes of the half and at the end of the game. When there are just two minutes left in each half, there is an official time-out called the two minute warning. After this time-out, there are a number of different things that might happen depending on the status of the game at that point. See if you can understand the following examples of how situation com-bined with time dictate strategy.

1. The offense is leading in the game, so practices ball control, as described above, to prevent the other team from getting an oppor-tunity to score.

2. The offense is behind, therefore institutes the <u>two minute drill</u>. Some quarterbacks are especially adept at this strategy. The plays that have been planned for this eventuality have been practiced over and over before the game, so that everyone knows exactly what to expect. No huddle is used at the beginning of each play. When one play is over, the offensive players line up quickly in position to execute the next. These plays may be audibles or they may be a preset series memorized by the offensive players. It all happens so fast that sometimes it can leave the defensive team baffled. Well, in all candor, this sometimes leaves the offense baf-fled as well. You can see why this is also called the "hurry up" offense.

3. To guard against all the possible plays that could happen during this hurry up deal, the defense must be very clever. If the offense has a long way to travel to the goal line, they are likely to call some long pass plays, so the defense institutes a "prevent" defense. We will discuss this in more detail in the next chapter, but what it means is that fewer players are at the line of scrimmage with more defensive backs strewn about to defend against a touch-down from a long pass or a fortuitous running play that breaks through the line to the backfield.

4. Each team tries to save its 3 time-outs to mete out during the last two minutes of the game. Also, if a play goes out-of-bounds or there is an incomplete pass, the clock is stopped. Therefore, with a combination of hurry up offense, pass plays, out-of-bounds, and use of time-outs, the trailing team, who has possession of the ball, may stretch the last two minutes of the game into 15 minutes or more, controlling the clock to its advantage. It happens that way. Of course, the defense attempts to keep the play in-bounds, delays getting ready for the next play, and does not call any of its time-outs, so that the clock does not stop and time is used up.

5. And, if the offense is ahead and is performing ball control, the defense attempts to use its time-outs to keep the clock from running out and ending the game - - with a loss!

We began this section with the idea that each team tries to control time by saving its time-outs to be used expeditiously toward the end of the game. Besides these near-end-of-game strategies, time-outs are generally used only because some mistake or another has been made. Here are two such conditions.

The quarterback sees that something is amiss at the beginning of a play - that people on the defense are lined up threateningly or that people on his own team are lined up improperly or there are too many of his players on the field or something. He calls a time-out.

The quarterback may also call a time-out if a delay of game penalty is imminent. As explained in Chapter 6 on rules, depending on the circumstances, 25 or 40 seconds are allotted from the end of one play until the next must be underway. A delay of game penalty is called against the offense if this time is exceeded. To avoid this penalty, the quarterback may simply call a time-out. Both of these situations are considered mistakes because, as we pointed out, it is desirable to save one's time-outs to be used toward the end of the half.

Rules Effect Strategy

Though in the next chapter we discuss some simple basic plays - strategies of the game - understand that the game is not at all simple. Rather, it is complicated and very fluid. The rules of the game change regularly, and so must strategy. (To repeat, the rules will be discussed more fully in Chapter 6.)

For example, in 1994, two rules were changed to enhance the offensive aspects of the game so there would be more opportunity for action and as a result, more scoring. One of the new rules set the ball back to the 30-yard line for the kick off. It had formerly been set on the kicking team's 35-yard line. As kickers improved and kicked farther, more and more kicks landed in the end zone, causing a touchback so that the offensive possession began at the offense's 20-yard line. Thus, fewer run-backs were being attempted. The run-backs from the kick off are an exciting aspect of the game. It was hoped that this change would provide the opportunity for more of these runs to occur.

The second rule change was that if a field goal is attempted and failed, the defensive team gets the ball where the kick was attempted. The rule used to be that after a field goal attempt, the other team took the ball over on its own 20-yard line. Then the rule was changed. After a failed field goal attempt, the other team got the ball on the line of scrimmage where the play originated. Now the rule has been changed again. Recall we said that field goals were attempted under certain conditions from the 35-yard line or closer, with the actual kick taking place about 7 yards behind that. If the play began on the 35, simple arithmetic shows that the opposing team begins its possession with a 22 yard advantage as a result of rule changes. (From the 20-yard line to the 35-yard line is 15 yards, plus 7 beyond that.)

Another aspect of the rules with a strategic component is how to decide whether or not to accept a penalty. The consideration is, what puts the team at the greatest advantage? For example, for many infractions, the penalty includes automatically taking the down over. If the play on which there was a foul happened on the third down, it would be to the advantage of the defense not to have the down replayed, because now it is fourth down and the ball will be turned over to the defense on the next play.

Another example: the offense made a huge gain on the down where an infraction occurred early in the play and the down would be played over if they accepted the penalty. They would not accept the penalty because they now have first down and a better field position to begin the next series of plays. Again, the thinking is - - what puts the team to the best field advantage?

Strategic Kicking

We have learned about the methods of scoring; what constitutes a score, like a field goal. Three points. So, when does a team attempt a field goal? We partially explained that, too: generally on fourth down, or if there are only a few, say eight or fewer, seconds remaining in the first or second half, and if the team attempting the field goal is 35 or fewer yards to the opponent's goal line. Not so complex, huh? No, it wouldn't seem so, but really, there are many circumstances that call for strategic thinking regarding whether or not to try a field goal.

For example, it is fourth down and the ball is on the defense's 27-yard line. It's midway through the third quarter. The offense is behind by, say, two touchdowns and needs a yard for the first down. Do they attempt the field goal or try for the first down? They have almost a sure three points at this distance, they have more time left to make up the two touchdowns, but only a short distance to convert (to make the first down.) What do you think? Maybe their kicker has missed two field goal attempts already today. Maybe the team's best runner for these circumstances has a sore toe. Maybe the wind has been blustery, and the kicker would have to kick into it. Maybe the coach is having a bad hair day which, as we all know, makes the decision that much more difficult.

There are infinite numbers of situations of this kind where the coach has to make the decision about whether to try for the field goal, try for the few yards, or punt. The people on the field, in the stands and on the air continually second guess the coach in these situations.

Check out Figure 4:1 (remember, the scrimmage line changes) to find where everyone stands during a field goal attempt. Now, too, we've learned something more about circumstances under which they do it.

We talked about and explained a punt earlier (Fig. 4:2). A punt is used by the offense on the fourth down, when they are too far away to attempt a field goal, to set the opposition further down field in the other direction from where they'd like to be. A good kicker can punt the ball 40 or 50 yards and the really, really good kicker can send the ball out-of-bounds at the opponents one-yard line. That is where the other team's offense will begin their march to the goal they will be trying to reach.

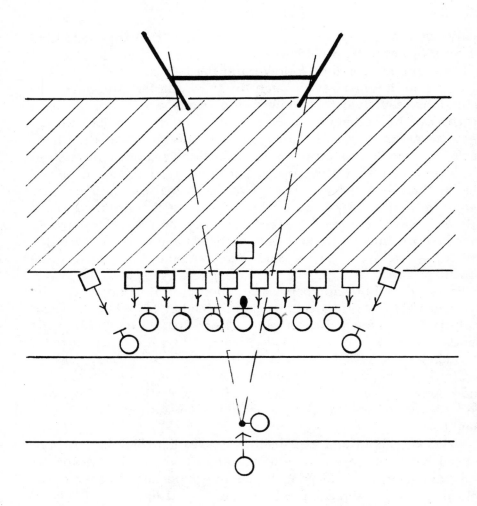

FIG. 4:1 POINT AFTER AND FIELD GOAL KICK

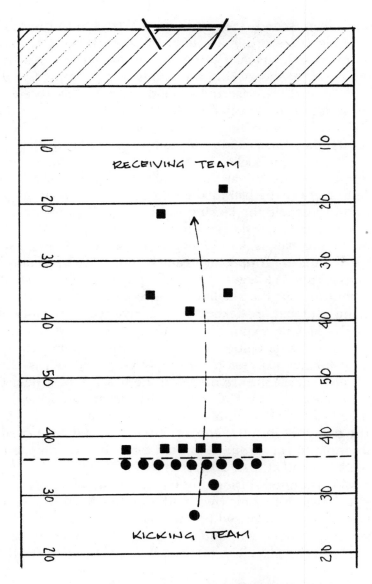

FIG. 4:2 PUNT CONFIGURATION

After a team scores, it must kick off (Fig. 4:3) to the other team, except when the score is a safety; then the team that was scored against must kick, usually punt, to the other team. As I said, the kick off begins at the kicking off team's 30-yard line. The ball must travel at least 10 yards to be valid, and if the receiving team touches it but does not catch it, the kicking team may grab the ball. Thus, if a team is trailing and has just scored and the game is nearing its end, the kicking off team may try an onside kick. The kicker intentionally kicks a short, rolling on the ground kick, traveling barely the 10 yard minimum, in hopes that his team may be able to recover the ball to keep the offense from running out the clock, and to enable the kicking team to catch up in the score. The onside kick is rarely used early in the game.

Usually the ball is kicked off as far as the kicker can kick it because it puts the opposing team in poor field position when it takes possession. However, unlike a punt, if the kicked ball goes out-of-bounds, out the sidelines, the receiving team has the option of having the ball rekicked with a five yard penalty assessed against the kicking team. On a normal kick off, that has traveled more than 30 yards before it goes out, the receiving team has the option of taking possession on the 40-yard line. As is true for so many issues, decisions are made on the basis of best field position. If the receivers opt for the rekick, the kicker, on second attempt, would be kicking off from his own 25-yard line.

If the ball goes into the end zone without being touched and no one attempts to run it out, it is then a touchback and the receiving team gets the ball at their 20-yard line.

We were stunned during one Eagles' game when Randall quick-kicked the ball out of his own end zone on third down. We were not the only ones surprised by this play. Randall, as you know, is a quarterback, not a kicker and it was still only third down. That is the beauty of the play. The offense, the Eagles, were clearly in

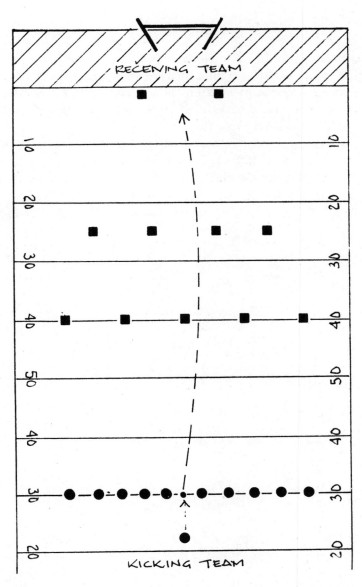

FIG. 4:3   KICK OFF CONFIGURATION

terrible field position. The defense, in this situation, might act in several ways, but they would not be likely to expect and prepare for this kick. A quick-kick, then, is a surprise kick that the defense would not expect and if effectively executed, should put the opposing team in unfavorable field position.

The considerations discussed in this chapter have been general ones regarding strategy. The next chapter describes a few basic plays/strategies more precisely and how exactly they work.

CHAPTER 5

BLUE 46. . .BLUE 46
HUT HUT, HUT

W hat appears on the field to the novice to be a chaotic mish mash of general mayhem and unconnected activity is, in reality, as carefully choreographed as a Balanchine ballet. As if linked to and part of a video game when the switch is turned on, each player knows exactly where he's to go, how many steps it will take to get there, and what he's to do when he arrives. Each of the 22 players on the field has an assignment. If you were flying high above in the Goodyear blimp, you could easily see it, just as you see the screen in the video game.

One correct joy stick jiggle will stop the forward progress of the villain on the screen. It is the charge of the defensive team to respond as to a joy stick in the same way, to anticipate what route the offense intends to sojourn and to be there ready to meet it.

Unlike the ballet, adjustments on the field are constant and instantaneous. The quarterback (QB) needs to be quick of mind and body. In terms of athletes, quick means fast, very fast in physical and mental reaction time. The defense, especially the linebackers and backs, also need to be quick to fill those holes, out-run and out-smart those runners and pass receivers, to render the offense impotent, I believe is how we stated it before.

Traditionally we have thought of jocks as being air heads, non-thinking, devoid of an original thought and so on. Genetically, these men are physically superior; why, then, would they also be dull? It makes no sense and in fact it is not so. Generally, players have focused less on the academic and more on the athletic, it takes that kind of dedication to make it, but that doesn't suggest that they are all innately stupid. The point is, understanding, memorizing, and executing the strategies on the field takes brain power. I think you will be surprised at how complex the game of professional football really is.

The Coaches

Uncle Marino has helped me with some of the nuances of the game. One of his letters to me said the following:

"I want you to know, the final vote on all-time great football coaches is in - - the results are:
Pro-football: Vince Lombardi of the Green Bay Packers.
College football: Joe Paterno of Penn State.
High School football: [Uncle] Marino Rosellini of Marysville, CA.
We are all Italian and sex symbols."

This is the kind of expert advice I've been getting from Uncle Marino. As for his coach picks, he very well may be correct.

I talked about the choreography of the game. The coaches are the choreographers, the players. . . the dancers. The coaches are the real creative brains behind the team and successful coaches are equally successful with different teams, that is, with a variety of players and owners.

Playbooks and Plays

Each coach, along with his staff, creates a *Playbook* for his team. This book is the bible for the team because it describes in detail the unique language employed by the team, along with the plays, patterns, and positions to be utilized by the team. It is the respon-sibility of each player to memorize the *Playbook* and to keep it confidential. A large fine is assessed a player who misplaces his *Playbook*.

The *Playbook* numbers the <u>holes</u>. The holes define every block-ing assignment and set up every play that will be part of the team's repertoire. You will recall that it is the job of the offense to bump the opponents out of the way, just so, so that the runner may run between the people who have been knocked down. The spot where the runner runs through will be a <u>hole</u>. These holes or potential holes are numbered along the front line, and each team has a different numbering system. We're not going to concern ourselves with numbering holes, but we will diagram some plays for you so you can see how holes might develop.

Though there are a few basic themes, there are infinite variations on those themes seen in these *Playbooks*. In response to my ques-tions about "plays", Uncle Marino sent me a book entitled *Ray Graves' Guide to Modern Football Offense*. This was as complex a book as any I've ever opened on any subject; mathematics, psychology, computer science, anything. I could not believe the meticulous way the 230 pages described the minute details of coaching and preparing an offensive team. It was difficult making sense of it. Uncle Marino informs me that the wisdom in the book is still current and can be very helpful to someone who is striving for a deep understanding of the offensive aspects of the game.

Another book that I picked up at the library, *Game Plan: The Language and Strategy of Football*, written by John Riggins and John Winter, shows how plays are constructed from beginning to end. It contains pages from *Playbooks* and favorite plays from different pro teams. If you wish to learn more about offensive strategies, this is another good source.

I am not Ray Graves nor am I John Riggins. Still, I want to show you some basic offensive strategies/plays so that you can understand in a general way what the players are trying to do or supposed to be doing on the field. I will also show a few defensive strategies that are designed to keep the offense from doing what it is trying to do.

When selecting a play, the most important consideration is surprise, to catch the other team off guard and to execute on ideas and moves that the other team does not anticipate; to outsmart the opponents, both offensively and defensively. To accomplish this, the coach uses his skill, his ingenuity, his imagination and his experience to think up all sorts of schemes.

Offensive Plays

Through-the-Line Running Plays. There are a family of plays run from a modified T-formation (as shown in Figure 3:4) in which a running back is handed the ball by the QB and proceeds through one of the many possible holes created by the down linemen on the front line. The primary destinations of these through-the-line plays are through the center or between either of the guards or tackles, or tackles and ends. As you saw on the diagram of where the offensive players might stand, one of the ends is close in, the other stands further away from the main group on the line. Generally, the "strong side" is the side where the end plays in close. Coach Uncle Marino tells us that the most successful running plays are run off tackle.

The <u>dive</u> is one of this family. Each of the linemen has his assignment; he knows who he has to block to open the hole. For the dive play to be successful, first the hole must be created by the front line, then someone must be assigned to block the linebackers immediately adjacent to the hole so that the runner, after having been handed the ball by the QB and running through the hole, can break through to open field. In our diagram (Fig. 5:1) the linebackers are blocked by the center and an offensive back.

The <u>quarterback sneak</u>, also a dive play, is used when a few inches are needed for the first down or for the touchdown. The QB takes the ball and follows the center across the line for a short gain.

A v<u>eer</u> is another of this group. Again, the linemen have their assignments. This time there is general movement on the line to one direction, which makes the defense believe the play will develop that way. When the running back receives the ball from the QB he, too, begins in the direction that has been established as the flow of the play. But, before the play is fully developed he can change direction depending on what the defense is doing and go the other way, "against the grain." In our diagram (Fig. 5:2) the runner goes to the weak side of the line off right tackle.

A <u>draw</u> (Fig. 5:3) is yet another of the many variations on these themes. It is a particularly sneaky piece of work because it begins by pretending to be a pass play and is generally called when a pass play is expected. The QB receives the ball from the center and back-peddles into the pocket (see Fig. 5:7 for pocket) as he would for a pass play, "drawing" the defensive players to him as they attempt to keep him from successfully passing the ball. In the meantime, the offensive linemen are blocking their special friends

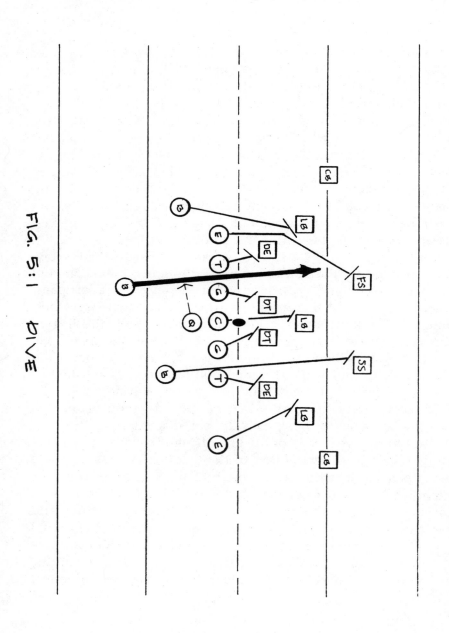

FIG. 5:1   DIVE

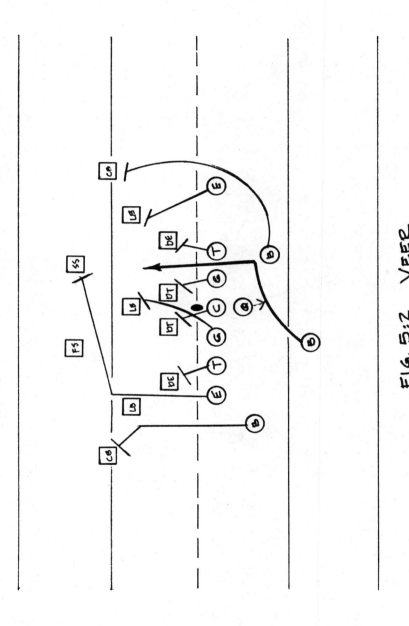

FIG. 5:2 VEER

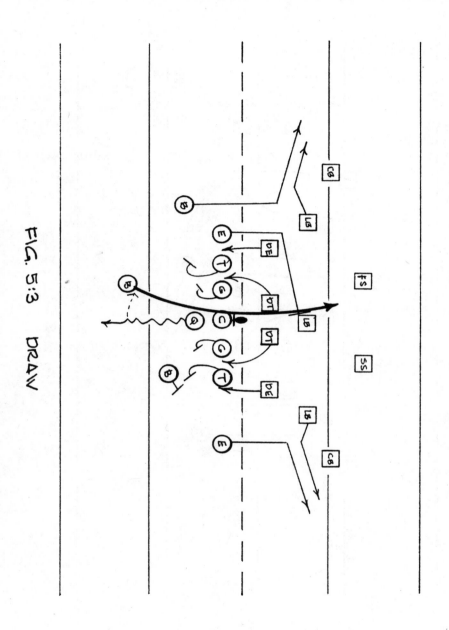

FIG. 5:3 DRAW

across the line in the way usually prescribed by a pass play, and the line-backers are falling back in their territory to defend against the expected pass. Instead of passing, the QB hands the ball off to a running back who runs forward through one of many holes opened at the line of scrimmage because the defensive linemen have been drawn off their usual routes.

As is true of every other play, the running back with the ball knows pretty much where he will be going though he can make choices as the play develops. Soon the linebackers will catch on to the deception and come back in. Someone will be assigned to block them before they get to the ball carrier.

Around-the-End-of-the-Line Running Plays. A <u>sweep</u> is one of the many types of plays that goes around the outside of the line. It is a quickly developing play which used to be referred to in college as "Student Body Right!" because the whole offensive team seems to be running around to the right. A running back blocks a defensive tackle, the center blocks the other defensive tackle, thus both offensive guards can pull out and run to the right to lead the way for the running back who has the ball, having received the hand-off from the QB. In our diagram, the party all runs - - sweeps around the right side of the line. (Fig 5:4)

A <u>pitch out</u> is set up by a fake hand-off from the QB to an offensive back. The QB then laterals, pitching the ball under-handed and across to another running back who runs outside and around the line with the ball. In our diagram (Fig. 5:5) the split end blocks the defensive left end, and the right offensive tackle blocks the left linebacker, which opens up a path around end for the running back. The initial fake hand-off sets the defense up to be looking for the play to go to the other side, either around or through the line.

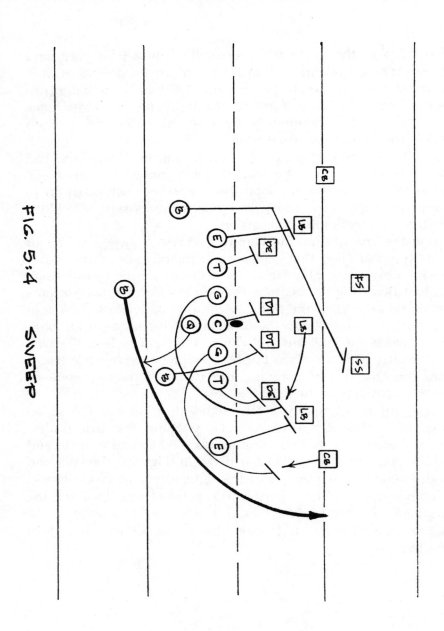

FIG. 5:4   SWEEP

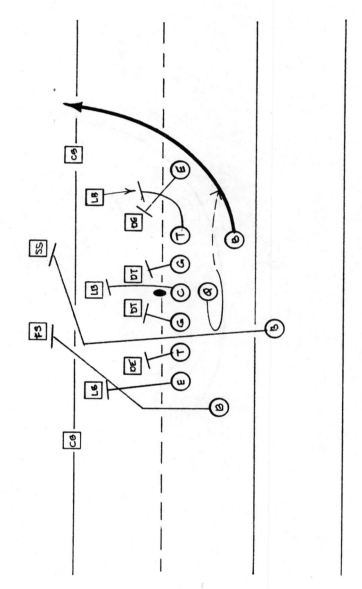

FIG. 5:5   PITCH OUT

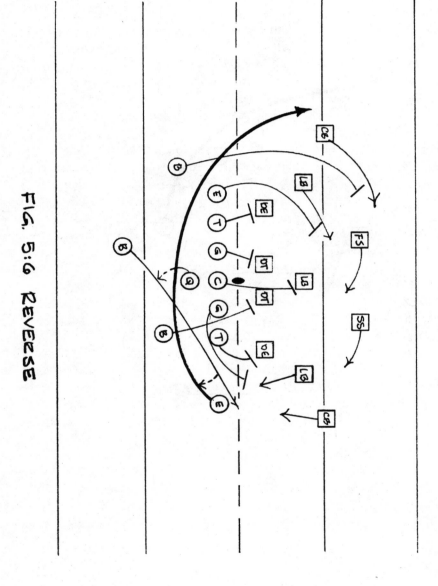

FIG. 5:6 REVERSE

A reverse is really tricky. The QB hands off to a running back who in turn hands it off to the split end who reverses the field, runs all the way to the other side and around the end of the line. Our diagram (Fig. 5:6) has the action beginning toward the right side of the line, then reversing to the left and around. Other players besides the end could be handed the ball and do the reversing. The play begins looking like a sweep to the right, setting the defense to moving toward its left and confusing them at least for the moment.

Passing Plays. Pass plays use either the modified "T-formation" mentioned above, or "Shotgun" formation. The QB either back-peddles into the passing pocket (Fig. 5:7) after receiving the ball from the center, or he is already standing about 7 yards behind the center (Fig. 5:8) to start the play. The center hikes the ball and the pass play begins.

There are three main receivers: the split end, the flanker back and the tight end. Each of these has an established set of patterns or routes he might run for any given play. Our diagram (Fig. 5:9) shows the patterns for the right end, who in our scheme of things, is also the split end, on the weak side. This person and the flanker back are also called wide receivers. (The preeminent pass receiver for the Forty-Niners, Jerry Rice, is a split end of the sort we are describing here but his patterns are likely much more complicated.)

Two or three receivers are running routes as per the instructions given them in the huddle. The tight end may block someone, then go out and run a pattern. The remaining two backfield players provide a kind of safety net for the QB. If everyone who has run his pattern is substantially covered by the defense, the QB might dump off the ball to one of the remaining backfield players. The backs who have not run out in a pass pattern generally stay around helping to protect the QB while he is preparing to pass, then they

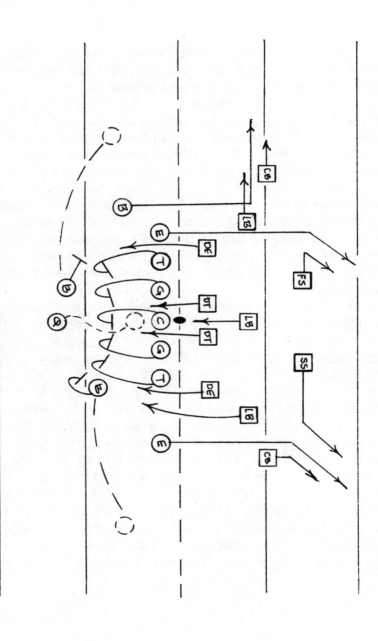

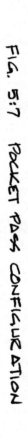

FIG. 5:7 POCKET PASS CONFIGURATION

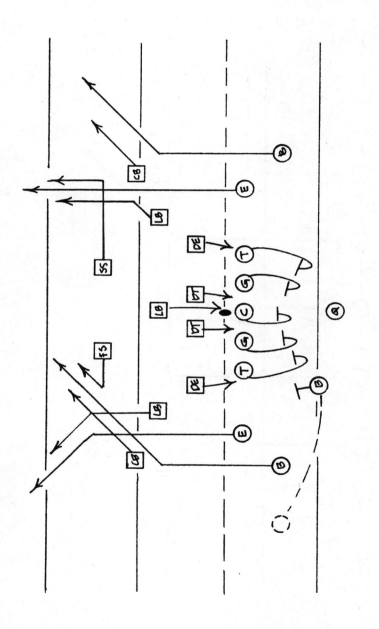

FIG. 5:B SHOTGUN PASS CONFIGURATION

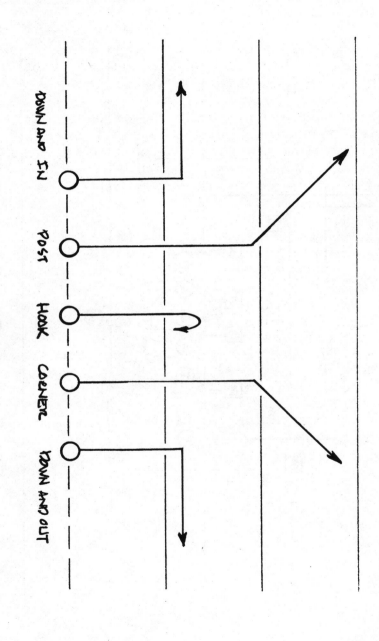

FIG. 5:9 PASS RECEIVER RUNNING ROUTES (RIGHT SIDE ROUTES SHOWN)

DOWN AND IN

POST

HOOK

CORNER

DOWN AND OUT

move off to the <u>flat</u>, to the outside of the play, near the line of scrimmage where the QB can throw the ball to them if need be.

The Patterns/Routes. The patterns in Figure 5:9 are designed to gain at least first down yardage. Passing routes are either to the inside, to the outside, in front of, or beyond the defensive backs. Remember, these routes are drawn for a right split end.

The <u>hook</u> takes the receiver from 5 to 15 yards past the line of scrimmage and in front of the defensive backs where he then turns around to face the QB to wait for the pass. Actually, there's not much stopping and waiting, it all happens very fast. (Then he catches the ball and runs, attempting to avoid the defensive back-field players who run real fast, on toward the goal line for the TD!)

<u>Down and in</u> takes the receiver beyond the linebackers, a little farther out than the hook, and then he turns straight in toward the middle of the field. (Then he catches the ball and runs, etc.)

<u>Down and out</u> takes the receiver beyond the linebackers, a little farther out than the hook, and then he turns straight out toward the sidelines. This is effective during the two-minute drill when the offense is behind and wants to stop the clock. The receiver can catch the ball, then run out of bounds, stopping the clock.

The <u>post</u> pattern takes the receiver beyond the linebackers, out among the defensive backs and beyond, angling to the left toward the goal posts. (Then he catches the ball and runs, etc.)

The <u>corner</u> pattern takes the receiver beyond the linebackers, out among the defensive backs and beyond, angling to the corner of the end zone. This will keep him the farthest away from the backfield defenders. (Then he catches the ball and runs. You get the picture!)

A Couple of Pass Plays. The <u>screen</u> play is a surprise play charac-terized by the offensive linemen allowing the defense to penetrate toward the QB, while they pull out to provide blocking for the running back. The QB throws a quick, short pass to the running back who is in the flat. The offensive guard, tackle and tight end provide a wall of blocking so that the runner can make good yardage after he has received the pass. This play is often used to soften the defense - that is, if the defense has been rushing the QB hard, they may not be so anxious to do so after a successful screen pass. (Fig. 5:10)

The roll-out pass is a play about the QB leaving the pocket and "rolling out"- - running out toward the sideline to execute the pass. This makes it necessary for the defense to pursue the QB and provides more time for the wide receivers to run their patterns down field. In our Figure 5:11, we show the roll-out preceded by a fake to a back, then the QB rolling to the weak side.

Audibles and Options. There are plays that begin as one thing and end up as another. If, for example, the QB calls for a play in the huddle, then as the offense is setting up, sees that the play is unlikely to work because of the way in which the defense is set up, he may call a new play at the line of scrimmage. This is called an audible, where the QB shouts some code words to his team, signifying a change to another play. The title of this Chapter might be an audible: "Blue 46. . . blue 46. . . hut hut, hut!"

And there are plays that give the QB a choice whether to pass or to hand the ball off to someone to run with it. These are called option plays. An attempt is made by the offensive line to isolate the linebacker on the side to which the play is being run. The linebacker then must make the decision to cover either the pass or the run, but is unable to do both. The QB has the option to hand the ball off, pass the ball, or pitch the ball out, depending on the decision made by the linebacker.

Unusual Plays. There are many ways to create unusual plays and they are often extremely tricky. These fancy plays are seldom used, always fun to watch, and nearly always a surprise to the

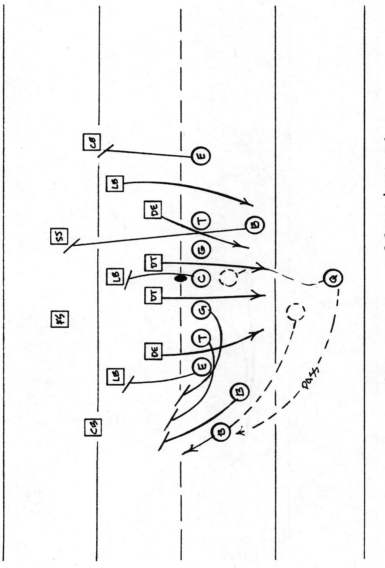

FIG. 5:10 SCREEN PASS

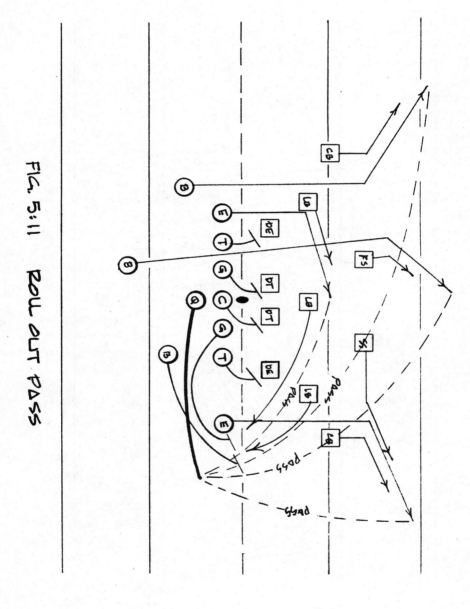

FIG. 5:11   ROLL OUT PASS

defense. Again, the creative coach can think up wild things to do with the ball.

One strange play is to have everyone go out for a pass, even sometimes including a guard, who is not allowed to do so without reporting his intention to the officials. This play, using the guard as a receiver, is rare and would most often happen near the goal line for a real surprise.

There is something called a halfback pass, where the QB hands off to a running back who then throws to a receiver down field. Of course, running backs are typically not known to be passers and the defense is expecting him to run, not to pull up and pass.

The flea flicker features the QB handing off to a running back, who then, as the play progresses, pitches it back to the QB who then passes it to a receiver down field. The defense thinks a running play is developing and focuses on the suspected runner. Surprise! The runner has returned the ball to the QB who is passing it down field.

A double reverse is where the QB hands off to one running back who proceeds to run across the field one way, then he hands the ball off to another running back, who runs back across the field the other way and around the end.

These kinds of plays take time to develop, which is one of the reasons they are rarely used. Quick moving, quick release plays are preferable. Also, in professional football, the defensive players are very clever and can usually see one of these types of plays developing.

Defensive Strategies

Defensive plays are more reactive than proactive. The defense will try to guess what the offense will do next, based on a number of considerations: how the game has gone thus far; which team is ahead; the type of talent on the offensive team (prime passer,

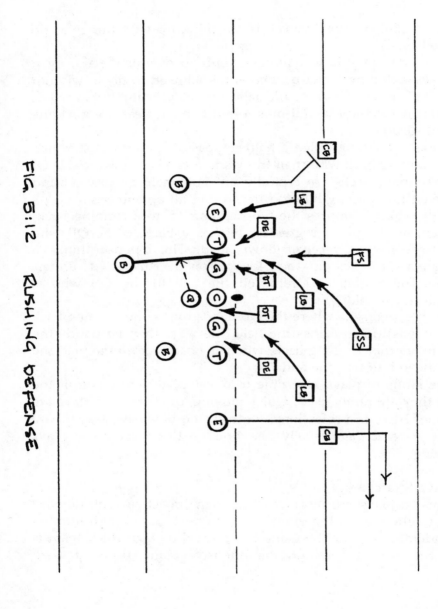

FIG. 5:12   RUSHING DEFENSE

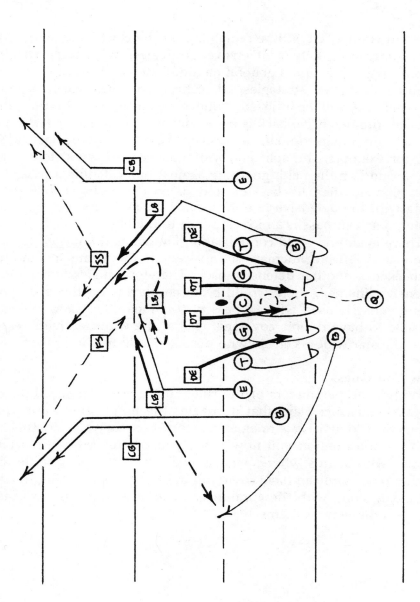

FIG. 5:13 PASSING DEFENSE

excellent runner, etc.); time remaining on the clock, and so on. We have diagrammed two defensive strategies, a general rushing defense (Fig. 5:12) and a general passing defense (Fig. 5:13).

Some defensive strategies are concerned with which type of pass defense will be utilized: zone or man-to-man. In the zone defense, the defensive back is responsible for a particular section of the field. In a man-to-man, he is responsible for a particular player, say, for example, the split end/wide receiver. He must follow his man around on the field, guarding against him catching a pass.

A blitz is when linebackers and defensive backs rush the QB along with the defensive line, trying for the sack. As we explained earlier, a screen pass is a nice response to the blitz.

There is another field configuration known as the nickel defense where a defensive lineman is replaced in the game by another linebacker or another defensive back. Therefore, instead of the four defensive linemen, there would be three players on the front line. This defense is used when a pass play is most likely and makes it possible to have double coverage against the wide receivers, especially the star wide receivers who pose a special threat.

Now You Guess

Within the parameters of the rules, there are so many different ways to construct plays that it boggles the mind. There are equal numbers of defensive strategies to stop those plays. Nonetheless, with the information you now have, you can tell who is blocking whom, who stands where, who is likely to run a pass route and catch a pass. You can have some fun guessing what's going to happen next, along with the announcers, the other fans, the coaches, and yes, the players themselves.

CHAPTER 6

RULES AND OTHER RELATED STUFF

A ll games must have rules, else the players will just run amuck and there will be game anarchy. There are behaviors and activities that are accepted and those that are not. These elements make up the game, the conditions and circumstances that describe what the people who are competing are expected to do in this contest. When we talk about "Rules" in professional football, we are talking both about what the game consists of - that is, how it's run - and what the players are expected to do. Actually, we are often talking more about what people are NOT allowed to do, rather than what they are expected to do.

Let me explain this concept further. There are in pro football, all those conditions that make up the game such as four tries to achieve 10 yards and so on. These are playing rules and are decided upon by God knows who at off season. Actually, it is a group of people called the <u>League</u>. (We believe this to be the Commissioner, Paul Tagliabue, the guy who is paid to run the League, and a committee comprised of some of the team owners.) This League makes decisions that it feels will enhance the game by making it more interesting, more fair, more safe, or all three.

For example, in 1987 the League decided that the field was too large and too much was happening at any one time for seven officials to be able to observe everything. To make the game more fair, an additional official was placed in a room with a TV monitor to monitor the play on the field. If there was a dispute regarding a call made by one or more of the officials on the field, a judgment could be requested by the teams or by the officials from the gentleman with the TV monitor who could watch instant replays of the incident in question. His judgment of the event stood, and the call on the field was adjusted accordingly. And, by the way, if the ball was put into play before a request to review was made, the chance to review was lost.

It seemed such a great idea at the time and certainly had its upside. Problem was, the time-outs required to rethink these calls were lengthy and delayed the game. Hence, this aspect of officiating, this experiment, was eliminated in 1992 after five seasons. Every year, there is still an on-going discussion as to the features and benefits of reinstating the replay official even though it was eliminated some time ago.

The League, before the 1994 season, made a couple of rule changes that had to do with play on the field and not with infractions during the play. Remember we talked about the new field goal rule that made attempting a field goal less attractive. And we talked about the new kick-off rule that enhanced the field position of the receiving team. These are playing rules and have little to do with personal infractions. The playing rules have been explained throughout this book, and are what the game is made of.

A Game of Inches

In Chapter 3, the importance of the seven officials to the conduct of the game was explained. The chapter also described a little about where they stand and what their specific duties are. Some of the things that the officials are responsible for include, for example, spotting (placing) the ball correctly on the field after the play, so that the next play will begin at the exact right place. As has been pointed out elsewhere, football is called a game of inches, (well, actually, I said this was a game of people rather than a game of inches) and where the ball is placed after a play ends is crucial to the success of the offense.

As I was reading other people's books about football, I read at least two different stories about how, in crucial games, the ball was (allegedly) spotted in the wrong place by the officials, denying the offense the first down that was essential to them winning the game. In his book, *I'm Still Scrambling*, Randall Cunningham tells a story about an incident during a San Francisco 49ers - Philadelphia Eagles game. The score is 20 to 14. The game is down to one play- - in football language: "fourth and 15 from the 26 with :53 seconds to play." Coach Kotite calls a pass play to the right. All of Cunningham's receivers seem to be covered, but Calvin Williams gets open, sort of. In Randall's own words:

> There was a guy on Calvin, but I thought I could sneak it in to him, so I fired it. Calvin made a great catch and it looked like he was tackled right at the 10 which should have been enough for the first down.
>
> I was sure we had the first down, so I start sprinting up to the 10, thinking we'd line up fast and I'd spike the ball into the ground to stop the clock. . . Then, as I'm running

toward the line of scrimmage, I can see there's all sorts of confusion. First of all, there wasn't a referee anywhere near Calvin when he caught the ball. One referee runs over and takes the ball and marks the spot with his foot. Where he marked it would have been a first down. Then another referee comes running up and takes the ball and puts his foot down to mark the spot. I could see this spot was six inches behind the first spot and I got worried. The first referee looked at the first down marker and saw how close it was and kind of walked away, like he was saying, "I'm not getting involved in this." . . . It was so close the referee had to kneel down and put his eye right up to the pole. . . The referee signals it's San Francisco's ball. . . Then Steve Young did a very smart thing. He ran out on the field and picked up the ball and put it back down. [Now] the referees couldn't remeasure the ball even if they wanted to.

This little vignette demonstrates how important the job of spotting the ball correctly is to the game.

The Official Sign Language

During a game, you will see officials making strange gestures and signs on the field, a kind of sign language, so that they can communicate what's going on to all concerned: players, coaches, other officials, and spectators. All this arm swinging and belly patting (not really), therefore, has significant meaning. Besides these signals, the referee, the main official, also explains what's happening through a cordless microphone he carries around on the field.

Some of the signals have to do with scoring and forward progress, some with the timing of the game, time in, time-out, begin, etc. Many signals have to do with fouls and penalties, to indicate that someone has done something he is not allowed to do.

A Score Is Awarded

In a prior chapter, we explained that there are four, well, five possible ways to score. Being a good student, you surely remember what these are. Following are the signs made by the officials telling the teams and everybody else that this particular score has been made.

Touchdown - 6 points: Both hands above the head, palms facing each other in a kind of "U" configuration.

Field Goal - 3 points: Same

Point or Points after touchdown - 1 or 2 points: Same

Safety - 2 points: Hands above the head palms touching.

Forfeiture - 1 point: There is no hand signal necessary for this circumstance, if it actually ever happens.

Forward Progress and Game Time

When a first down is awarded, the official stands, looking toward the defense's goal and sort of points toward the goal line, arm outstretched, with his whole hand palm inward, not just one finger like regular pointing.

Sometimes there is a question as to whether a pass has been legally caught; it might have hit the ground first and taken an almost imperceptible bounce, or the receiver might have stepped out-of-bounds before or while catching the ball. If it is ruled an incomplete pass, the referee, or field judge or someone (official), sort of leans over, bending at the waist and moves his hands and arms quickly back and forth across each other, signifying that this pass was not caught. If it is an actual reception, the ball is spotted where the play ends; that is, where the receiver's forward progress is stopped by the opposing team.

If, while running down the field, a player steps on or out of the sidelines, the referee points energetically to the sideline, expressing the point of view that the runner was out.

Often the play on the field is stopped to measure whether the offense has gained a first down or not. On the sidelines are two markers attached to a chain 10 yards long. The downs are also displayed on or next to the markers. When the ball has been placed at a certain spot on the field and the judges cannot tell whether the team has gained the whole 10 yards, the chain is called out to the ball, one end placed where the drive began or where the last first down occurred, the other next to the football. If the football sticks out even a smidgen beyond the marker pole, a first down is awarded. If the tip of the football is short of the 10 yard marker, play continues and a first down is not awarded. Sometimes the official will signal to the crowd how short the ball was to a first down, by signing with his fingers or both hands.

Time in or Out

At the beginning of the game or after a score or at the beginning of the second half, the ball is kicked off to the opposing team. Before this can happen, the referee blows his whistle to signal the start. He also whistles to signal the resumption of the game after a time-out. Besides whistling, the referee usually swings one arm in a windmill-type fashion. This signal gets the clocks started.

One of the officials also blows his whistle to signify the end of the play, thus the play stops, the ball is whistled "dead".

Any player for either team may call time-out by forming a "T" with his hands toward an official. Each team, as was explained earlier, is allotted three 2-minute time-outs for each half.

Fouls and Penalties

There are aplenty. Remember, there is a very nice *NFL Rule Book* that details all the various rules, fouls, and penalties of the game. I'm going to describe the most common, along with the signals the officials make to let everyone know what the foul is and what penalty shall be meted out.

It is important to know that the team that had the infraction committed against it can decline the penalty. In many cases, if the penalty is accepted, the down is played over. Part of the strategic thinking of the game is to decide when to accept or reject a penalty. For example, if it is third down, depending on the nature of the foul and the yardage to be penalized, chances are the defense would not want the down played over. Without the penalty, it becomes fourth down and the offense will probably have to turn the ball over to the defense by punting. The official sign for refusing the penalty is the referee moving his hands palm down, low, back and forth across each other. (This also signals incomplete pass and no score.)

Another strategic consideration is when both teams commit fouls on the same play. If the ball did not change hands on the play and depending on the severity of the respective fouls, the two infractions will often offset each other so that neither team is punished. The officials decide about these things.

While at any given point in time, people closely associated with the game will have a good grasp of the rules, I think we've made the point indirectly that the rules are a point of some fluidity. That is, the League changes the rules annually and furthermore, the language changes. What is called "encroachment" one season by the coaches, players, and announcers, may be called "territory embargo" or some other nonsense in the next season.

Nonetheless, one of the books I've been using was published in 1972. Many of the rules are the same, many of the officials' signals are the same. So certain general concepts maintain constant over the years. If not, if one pays attention, the major changes, such as the "instant replay" rule will get discussed over and over again. You will be informed of the changes.

Some of the most frequently called infractions or fouls that require a penalty or punishment are discussed in the next section. The referee's signal and the associated penalties and awards are also described.

Most Frequently Called Fouls

At the beginning of each play, there are several different possible infractions that can occur at the line of scrimmage as things are getting underway. These are: offside, illegal motion, encroachment, and false start.

Offside and encroachment: Both hands on hips.

An offside penalty is awarded when a player is over his line of scrimmage when the ball is snapped. A defensive player may jump offside but if he touches no one and returns to his own side before the ball is snapped, no penalty is called. Encroachment is when the player jumps over the line and touches a member of the other team before the ball is snapped.

Penalty/award: Five yards.

Illegal motion and false start: One arm crossing chest, hand down, making a forward motion. And, a tumbling circular motion of both hands.

One man is allowed to be in motion away from the scrimmage line. If that player moves toward the scrimmage line or if two players start in motion, that is illegal motion. Once the offensive down linemen are set, (that is, crouched in a three-point position with two feet and one hand on the ground,) they are not allowed to move at all until the ball is snapped. They may not sneeze, look from left to right, they are not supposed to move. This kind of movement makes the defense believe the play has begun and pulls players offside. It is often hard to see who first commits the infraction at the line of scrimmage but the official known as the

Linesman (not to be confused with the linemen) takes care of all that.

Penalty/award: Five yards.

There are a number of rules related to pass plays and infractions for some of these can be very expensive.

Pass Interference: Two spread hands pushed forward, arms bent at elbow.

When an end or backfield person is down field and expecting to make a pass reception (catch), the defending team may not bother him physically, that is touch or bump him. A new rule allows the defensive player to guard the intended receiver as one might in basketball, with his back to the ball, as long as there is no contact.

There may be some incidental contact and if the defending player is watching and going for the ball, interference will probably not be called. Also, interference is not called if the ball is deemed uncatchable, if both players are interfering with each other, or if the intended receiver is already out-of-bounds. Once the ball is touched or even tapped as it flies through the air, anyone can push anyone to get a chance at catching it.

Offensive pass interference is where the offensive player bothers the defensive player physically instead of going for the ball.

Penalty/award: For defensive pass interference, the ball is placed where the infraction occurred, as if the pass had been completed there, and an automatic first down is awarded. If the infraction happens in the end zone, the next play begins at the one-yard line.

Offensive pass interference is a 10 yard penalty. That means that the ball is placed 10 yards behind where the pass play began.

Illegal Contact: Right hand spread, pushed forward, arm bent at elbow.

Related to pass interference, a defensive player bumping or blocking a potential pass receiver once while they're within five yards of the line of scrimmage is fair. However, this same sort of bumping done twice or past five yards is illegal contact, even though the ball may not have yet been thrown.

<u>Penalty/award:</u> Five yards and an automatic first down.

Illegal Man Down Field: Right hand patting top of head.

Some rules are established so that one team does not have an advantage over another. Apparently, if a lineman, who would not ordinarily go out for a pass, goes down field past the line of scrimmage, past the defensive line player he blocked, and looks like he might be trying to catch a pass, the defensive team has too many men to cover and becomes confused. Therefore, this is illegal with the exception of the play where the guard reports to the officials that he intends to go out for a pass. (Go figure!)

<u>Penalty/award</u>: Five yards.

Many of the rules associated with the game have to do with personal fouls or being unnecessarily rough or rude on the field, in a way which jeopardizes the health of the players on the other team. Some of these are <u>roughing the passer or kicker,</u> <u>grabbing a face mask,</u> <u>unnecessary roughness,</u> <u>tripping,</u> <u>clipping,</u> and <u>illegal use of hands</u>.

Roughing the passer or kicker: Hands above head, crossed, left in fist, right in chopping motion (the signal for personal foul) followed by a small kick motion with the foot or a passing motion with the arm.

After the kicker has kicked the ball, the defensive team may not, under most circumstances, run into him and knock him down.

Likewise, after the pass has been released, the defenders must try to avoid knocking down the quarterback. If the defender touches the kicked ball, then bumps the kicker, that is allowed. Also, if the momentum of the defender takes him into the passer, this foul will perhaps not be called.

<u>Penalty/Award</u>: 15 yards, automatic first down. Incidental roughing the kicker, 5 yards.

Face Mask: Clinched fist in front of the face, moved up and down.

All players wear face protection in the form of bars attached to their helmets. These are called face masks. No player may grab the face mask of an opposing player. The potential resultant injuries can be very serious. If a player just grazes another's face mask but lets go immediately, this is considered incidental. But when the face mask is held and used as an instrument to get the other player down, this is considered flagrant and is much more serious.

<u>Penalty/Award</u>: Incidental - 5 yards. Flagrant - 15 yards, automatic first down.

Unnecessary Roughness: Hands above head, crossed, left in fist, right in a chopping motion - personal foul.

This occurs on several different occasions such as, when the player is obviously down and a defensive player piles on, or when the player is already out-of-bounds and the defense tackles him - anything where gratuitous violence is perpetrated against another player.

<u>Penalty/Award</u>: Against defense, 15 yards and first down. Against offense, 15 yard loss. If, in the view of the official, this was a real awful infraction, the player may be ejected from the game. Disqualified. The old heave ho - - signaled by a thumb moved in a manner such as one might use in hitching a ride. You're outa' here!

Tripping: Personal foul sign. Small kick motion with foot.

Players are not allowed to stick out their feet and trip one another, including the ball carrier.

Penalty/Award: 15 yards from the spot of the infraction.

Clipping and Illegal Use of the Hands: Personal foul sign. Chopping sign to behind the knee.

Both clipping and illegal use of the hands signify improper blocking. One may not block another player from behind. Below the waist is clipping, above the waist is illegal use of the hands. These infractions generally are not called close to the center of the line of scrimmage when the play was recently begun.

Penalty/Award: Clipping; 15 yards. Illegal use of hands; 10 yards

There are a variety of other kinds of rules and infractions in the game.

Delay of Game: Two arms crossed, extended, shoulder high.

There is a time limit for how long the offense can dally between plays. This is 40 seconds from the end of the last play. Or, if the clock has been stopped for some reason, 25 seconds after the officials call time-in again. That is, the center must hike the ball before the time limit expires. If play does not commence on time, a penalty is levied. If the QB sees that time will expire and his team has time-outs left, he has the option of calling a time-out to avoid the penalty. This, again, is all part of the game strategy.

Penalty/Award: 5 yards.

Intentional Grounding: Open parallel hands moved diagonally across the front of the body.

We have talked before about the sack, where the defensive players tackle the quarterback before he is able to pass the ball. If he leaves the pocket- you know, that little stretch of turf from seven to ten feet behind the line of scrimmage where his team mates line up around him to protect him - the quarterback may throw the ball to no apparent receiver, to avoid being sacked. If he is still in the pocket, he may not throw the ball away in this fashion, for if he does, he will be called for intentional grounding.

Penalty/Award: 10 yards, or where the infraction occurred, which ever is greatest.

As with some other infractions, if this occurs in the QB's own end zone, a safety is awarded. Two Points for the opponents! And they also get the ball kicked to them.

Also, there is this strange rule where the quarterback may down the ball to stop the clock if time is running out in a half. In this contingency, the center snaps the ball and the quarterback immediately spikes it into the ground. Intentional grounding will not be called in this eventuality.

Offensive/Defensive Holding: Left wrist held by right hand in front of chest.

Holding means constricting a player other than the ball carrier by encircling him with hands and arms or grabbing an arm or a jersey. Most often, this infraction is committed by the offensive line in its attempt to knock the defense out of the way. It also happens when a defensive player holds onto an offensive back who might be trying to catch a pass. If the offense is called for holding behind its own goal line, a safety is awarded the defense. Two Points! Plus, you will remember, the team that won the safety gets the ball kicked off to them.

Penalty/Award: Offensive holding - 10 yards. Defensive holding - 5 yards.

Unsportsmanlike Conduct: Arms outstretched to each side, shoulder high, palms down.

Even though the people on the field are banging and smashing into each other and tossing each other to the ground, players are not allowed to swear or insult one another excessively. Neither can they swear at the officials, coaches, or teammates. I doubt they are allowed to fuss at fans either. Punching or kicking opponents or faking being hit illegally by an opponent are all cause for being called for unsportsmanlike conduct. Recall we also mentioned that undue celebration after a sack or a touchdown is also cause for penalty, though this is not as serious an infraction as the other behaviors. Because these things may be personal fouls, players may also be disqualified or ejected for the more serious infractions.
Penalty/Award: 15 yards. Celebration - 5 yards.

There are many more fouls and penalties than those we have described here. Some are quite fun, like leaping, which is standing on the back of another player to block an attempted field goal or point after touchdown. Hurdling, some variety of jumping over other players, is also not allowed. There is something called illegally touching the ball. I think this prohibits an ineligible receiver, such as a lineman, from reaching up and touching or catching the ball. And if the receiver first steps out-of-bounds, then back in, he may not then catch the ball; this, too, would be illegally touching the ball.

I said it several times before, it is possible to obtain an *NFL Rulebook* to find out about all the rules and regulations. I did not. The infractions and penalties aspect of the game can be highly confusing and complicated. I have attempted to supply you with enough information to enable you to assess the calls as they occur from the officials. You will not agree with them all. You will want to yell at the officials. You are allowed to do this because you are now beginning to become a fan.

CHAPTER 7

FINDING AND SIGNING THE TALENT

How do the teams get their players? In each of the big-time professional sports, an attempt is made to effect parity, which means that the teams approach equivalence in their ability to win games. The way teams get their talent is based on this notion of fairness and parity. In professional football, players are acquired by teams in several different ways: the college draft, trades, free agency, and some teams hold a try-out camp where the also-rans can come to show their stuff. Most of the latter come from colleges around the country who the scouts have been watching. In all, the National Football League teams are looking for, count 'em, about 1,500 really good players!

The Draft

I'm writing a book about football, right, and the college draft is an important aspect of the game, so, on April 22, 1995, I spent the better part of the day watching the 60th Annual college draft broadcast on ESPN. I was fully prepared to sneer and be cynical about this event which could be likened to a slave auction, but almost immediately I was engaged and had a wonderful time watching the proceedings.

There is a guy, Mel Kiper, Jr., whose main thing is the draft. He publishes a book about it and his prognostications are in newspapers and magazines across the country. I had picked up *Inside Sports* a few weeks earlier and had read about Kiper's ratings of the college seniors, who the best players were and so on. How he became the guru of the draft is one of the mysteries that will not be revealed; I simply don't know. He was one of the gentleman announcers bringing this day to us over Channel 36.

Along with Guru Kiper, Jr., was Chris "Boomer" Berman. If you have ever watched, which of course you haven't, during football season, the ESPN recap of the day's professional football happenings at 9:00 PM in California, you will understand why this man is nick-named Boomer. He personifies the excitable sports announcer whose voice reaches a crescendo with the touchdown or the home run. He clearly loves what he does and enjoys getting the viewing audience involved. He is fun.

Joining the Guru and the Boomer at the broadcasters' desk was Joe Theismann, former quarterback for the Washington Redskins. He is knowledgeable, good looking and also interesting to watch.

Besides these three guys, there were assorted correspondents stationed around the country - - many of whom were also named Chris. There were even two women among them.

The event was held in the huge Paramount Theatre in New York City. There was a podium next to a long table where team representatives hovered over their telephones and who were identified by the helmets placed in front of them on the table. I could not tell whether they were located on the premises or all over the country, but somewhere there were rooms referred to as "war rooms" where men in ties, having removed their suit coats, had boards where they monitored who had been taken, what kind of players they needed, and among those who remained, who would fit best into their programs.

Apparently, these men (I saw no women as part of this process) had planned for months for this day, and are tearing their hair out watching and telephoning other war rooms, making deals, and sending orders to their reps on the floor. There is a high degree of secrecy practiced in all this. It tends to remind one of the selection of a new pope, when the signal of white or gray smoke is emitted from the chamber where the solemn selectors are gathered.

In the rafters of the theater were a few seats reserved for the fans. Since this event was held in New York, these were primarily Giants and Jets fans. We did espy a few yellow terrible towels, so some Pittsburghers made it to the occasion, too.

Out in front of the theatre was a little blues band, dressed in black T-shirts with ESPN Draft lettered in white on their fronts. We were given only glimpses of the outside music which had a wonderful woman vocalist, but it added to the festivities nonetheless.

Damn! It was exciting. A book's worth of drama - - one chapter of space.

Understand that the draft is set up in an order calibrated by a complex formula related to last season's win/loss records. New players are selected from the pool of just-about-to graduate college seniors and others who have decided to forego their college programs to become professional football players.

Before the two days of the draft were over, 249 picks were going to be made in about seven rounds of picking. Paul Tagliabue, the Commissioner of Football announced the picks and trades. Some teams traded their turn in the rotation for later picks or players. The Commissioner came to the podium, announced the pick of the team whose turn it was, then announced that the next team "Is on the clock". Each team had 15 minutes to decide who it would select.

Here's the rub. There are probably only 15 to 30 really, really good college players who will clearly succeed in professional football. Only about a handful of these will be Pro-Bowl players. (Where the best are picked at the end of the season to have a game against each other.) There are 30 teams. It's obvious that some teams may want the same players. If a team sees its number one pick being picked, its representatives must go back to the drawing board and within 15 minutes reassess their position.

There were two new expansion teams in 1995, the Carolina Panthers and the Jacksonville Jaguars; these were given first and second pick in the first round.

When the Commissioner got up to announce the first pick, he announced that Carolina had traded its first pick to the Cincinnati Bengals for their 5th and 32nd spots. The Commissioner then announced that the Bengals picked Ki-Jana Carter, Guru Kiper, Jr.'s number one player, along with, it seems, everyone else's.

"Jacksonville is on the clock."

Ki-Jana Carter is a running back from Pennsylvania State who had 1,530 rushing yards, 23 touchdowns plus 3 in the Rose Bowl, and averaged an astonishing 7.8 yards per carry. He is 5'10" and weighs 227 pounds.

Next, Jacksonville picked Tony Boselli, a University of Southern California (USC) offensive tackle. He was said to be a wonderful all-around person, with a 3.02 GPA. This young man is 6'6" and weighs 325 pounds - one of the biggies I have described before. This, for reasons I could not divine, was a surprise pick according to the announcers.

And the Oilers picked Steve McNair, quarterback from Alcorn State. The Redskins picked wide receiver Michael Westbrook from University of Colorado. Carolina picked quarterback Kerry Collins from Penn State with the 66.7% completion rate, a take-charge kind of person. The St. Louis Rams (the Rams were allowed to move after all) picked Kevin Carter, a huge defensive end from Florida.

Now, in the telling, it seems all very straight forward, but. . .the drama was brewing. On the night before the draft, Chris Mortensen for ESPN had broken the story that the young man generally considered the second most desirable draftee had failed at least seven drug tests during his college years; six for marijuana and one for cocaine. The report had come from the NFL committee that supposedly monitors these things.

Each time a pick was made, the TV camera panned to Warren Sapp, the excellent defensive tackle from Miami University. Chris Berman called him the best player in the draft, yet there he sat, hour after hour, no one picking him. Commentators, one after another, sang his praises: explosive off the ball, always knows what's going on, the best defensive player around.

Sapp, at 6'1", weighs 280 pounds. What should have been one of the most exciting days of his life was turning into a nightmare because of what his manager called a lot of false accusations about drug use from the NFL and from the media. At last, as the cameras zoomed in, the call came from Tampa Bay. He would be their choice. Over the phone, Warren promised Coach Wyche that he would make good their choice and belie the rumors. In the 12th round, the first or second best player was picked.

So back to pick #7, which belonged to Tampa Bay. Now pay attention: Tampa Bay used all its 15 minutes to trade its #7 pick to

Philadelphia for its 12th, 43rd, and 63rd (second round) picks. Philadelphia also got Tampa Bay's third round pick. Philadelphia, now making the #7 pick, picked Mike Mamula, a fine defensive end from Boston College. The Eagles' Coach Ray Rhodes said Mamula was exactly who they had wanted all along. Then when it was again Tampa's turn, at #12, they got Sapp, perhaps the first best player in the draft. There ya' go.

And the draft moved along. The Seattle Seahawks chose Joey Galloway, a wide receiver from Ohio State.

The Jets, in the 9th position, much to the chagrin of the rafter gallery, chose Kyle Brady, 6'6", 260 lb., tight end from Penn State. Even the announcers were aghast. This was the first real curve ball of the draft, the announcers said. The gallery heads were shaking, no! And booing loudly. I never understood quite why, except, remember, at this point, Mr. Sapp, the maybe best player in the draft, was still just sitting there.

Then it was Cleveland's turn at number 10. This was the biggest, most interesting deal of the day. Cleveland traded their #10 pick for, now pay attention again, 1st round 30th pick, 3rd round 94th , Kansas City's 119th, and San Francisco's 1st round pick in 1996. Did I mention how complex this is? Like a game of chess. And you've guessed by now who jumped in to take this #10 pick, the San Francisco 49ers, naturally. How do you think they win those Super Bowls? Who did they choose? Who was so important to give up four future picks?

J.J. Stokes, the wide receiver from UCLA! At 6'4" and 217 lb., this young man caught for 2,293 yards during his college career. Stokes was listed among the top five players in the draft. Kiper had him as number 3. As the announcers were ooing and ahing at this perfect utilization of the draft system, some commented on the *de ja vu* quality of the event. This is how San Francisco had obtained

Jerry Rice in 1986. (I mentioned in an earlier chapter how those Niners love those wide receivers.)

Boomer Berman said, "No pun intended. The Niners have struck gold!"

And the draft continued. Number 11, Minnesota picked Derek Alexander, a defensive end from Florida State, we told you about #12 Tampa Bay and Mr. Sapp, numbers 13, 14 and 15 made selections. The Jets had another 1st round pick because of trades and at #16 picked Hugh Douglas, a linebacker whom the people in the gallery did not even know, and again they were chagrined.

Then came #17, the New York Giants.

In the summer of 1994, I read a wonderful article in *Sports Illustrated* about Tyrone Wheatly, a running back from University of Michigan. I naturally fell in love. After his junior year, his agents got him a great deal - - $1.2 million for one year, $3.6 million for two, $8 million for four, a signing bonus, incentive clauses and endorsement deals. Tyrone just said no. The article took three interesting pages to explain and describe Tyrone, and the difficult life circumstances that have surrounded this fascinating young man. The upshot was, he wanted to demonstrate to his young brother Leslie that he meant it when he said education was more important than money. Tyrone stayed at University of Michigan to get a degree in education and waited until 1995 to participate in the draft. He plans to be a school administrator in special schools for special students with problems.

So, I know about Tyrone and there is a rumor all day that the LA Raiders might be interested. I am ecstatic. The Raiders could be considered my home team, located within 100 miles of where I live. But, pow! The Giants, with their #17 selection, picked my favorite, or so I thought. I was momentarily broken-hearted.

Then it was #18, the Raiders' turn. And they reached down deep. They picked my real #1 favorite, Napoleon Kaufman. The announcers were very surprised. Though Kaufman is good, a first round pick was really unexpected. As I searched Guru Kiper's lists in *Inside Sports*, I found no mention of Napoleon at all.

But I know him. For me, Napoleon is the closest thing to a bona fide home town hero. He went to high school in Lompoc, in Santa Barbara County. When he played in Lompoc, his teams were powerful, winning everything. And he was the 60-meter champion. He went from high school to the University of Washington where he had a very successful career. He amassed three years of 1,000 plus yard gains, 1,400 his last year. And he averaged 5.5 to 6.5 yards per carry. He can catch too. Studying tapes and spending time learning how to be better, Napoleon, as the announcers pronounced, has heart.

"I can't explain how excited I am." he was quoted as saying. Of course the local newspapers picked up the story about Napoleon and the draft. Again, a lovely picture was painted. Two quarters to finish, then he earns his college degree. He's happy to be a Raider and just wants to play ball to show what he can do. It's a wonderful moment for him. Being selected in the first round, 18th of the hundreds of other eligible players, is a great honor for a young foot-ball player.

And the drama continues. . . Napoleon was picked before last year's Heisman Trophy winner, Rashaan Salaam from Colorado, who sat around waiting and was finally selected by the Chicago Bears on the #21 pick.

More picks are made, more trades are negotiated. It began at 9:00 AM and by 3:30 PM, the announcers are exhausted and so am I. But the whole thing continues for the rest of this and the next day until all 249 picks are made.

The annual National Football League (NFL) draft is held in April each year. It is an event that has far reaching ramifications regarding the future success or failure of a team. I first heard about the draft and acquired an understanding about how it operates when my middle son, an avid New York Jets fan, followed the draft one year on TV. He hooted and howled and sizzled at the real or perceived bad judgment of the representatives from his favorite team. For him as for others, this occasion was similar to watching a game. There was definitely an aspect of winning, losing, imagined advantage and so on.

No one except the very most insiders from each team knows how a team has decided to choose, certainly not the selectees them-selves. And the future of a team can be contingent on the decisions and luck of this day. If one team takes another team's first choice, as we pointed out, the second team has only 15 minutes to deliberate and make a new selection. It can be gripping. Observers cheer. Some people look desperate.

The player will eventually negotiate a contract and ultimately decide whether he and the team will actually come to agreement, but a little like slavery, a player plays for the team that either selects or buys him.

Several years ago, I watched the draft transactions with interest as the rounds passed without any team selecting Rodney Peete, the talented star quarterback of the USC Trojans. This young man had been runner-up in the voting for the prestigious Heisman Trophy, had led his team to the Rose Bowl for two consecutive years, breaking record after record, yet, by the end of the fifth round, eight quarterbacks had been selected, none of whom was Rodney Peete. The draft was over for the day. Monday morning, finally, the Detroit Lions named young Peete to their team, in the sixth and final round of the process.

Quite the *brouhaha* ensued. Why hadn't Peete been selected earlier? On Sunday night, Peete's father, a pro football assistant coach, held a near-tearful press conference. He told how he had studied films of his son's performance and found him flawless in every regard, that he had great potential for a pro quarterback. The elder Peete seemed at a loss to explain the apparent snub to his son.

As the discussion continued, the black issue was raised. In all of pro football, at that time, there were only three starting black quarterbacks. (During the 1994 season there were only two.) No! Foul! Nonsense, cried the media. Football experts said this is a business, a big money business. A player could be black, red or purple and teams would buy him if they thought he could win games. At 6'1/2" and 190 pounds, Rodney Peete was small, not enough of a powerhouse. He had suffered injuries in recent games. Some questioned his staying power, others wondered about his arm; could he pass the ball consistently and capably? Rodney Peete's story was indeed an interesting one.

As the commotion died down, the consensus was that the team that finally chose Rodney, the Lions, was the best possible fit for him. They had a run n' shoot offense which Rodney was very well suited for. He played for the Lions with moderate success for a number of years.

In the 1994 season, Peete played back-up quarterback to Troy Aikman on the very successful Dallas Cowboy team. I don't know if anyone else watched his progress, but my guess is that good old boys from Southern California were very interested in how he faired. He was cute, likable and sort of an underdog. Lots of people thought he was poorly treated in the draft.

Rodney Peete's story and the others I have told here are exactly the sort that will get people interested in and rooting for a particular player. I don't know if Rodney will be back with the Cowboys. For your first fan assignment, look for him. (#9, I think!)

Free Agency and Trades

Another mystery is, what is this business about free agency? All thoughts and notions about purchasing players have been rendered completely incomprehensible with the onset of the salary cap. Let's see if I can explain it.

A player gets drafted. He and his business managers work to strike a deal with the owners of the team to whom he now belongs. He may not play nor practice with the team until this piece of business is completed. The backdrop for the negotiation is the salary cap. As you read in Chapter 1, the salary cap dictates a cumulative total dollar number that a team can pay for all its players. If the team and the player cannot strike a deal, the player may sit out a year and not play at all. Generally, though, the deal is made including a contract length, say three years.

During the three years, the relationship is successful or it is not. If it is not, the player may be released at any time by being placed on waivers. When a player is released, all other teams have 24 hours to claim him by paying him the salary the team paid who has released him. If he is not picked up he becomes a free agent. Unless he has a guaranteed contract, he then receives no further salary from his team.

The player may also be traded to another team for another player or players, or for draft picks. The new team presumably takes over the debt of his contract. After a contract has run its course, and if the relationship has been a good one, the team and player work on their next contract, and so it may go until the end of the player's career.

The more likely scenario is that the player will play with several teams throughout his career and at any point may be without a contract or a team. He is then a free agent and may negotiate with any team who is interested. Remember, though, it is not that a team just swoops down and buys a player. Negotiations are at all times constrained by the team's salary cap.

I believe what I have explained is close to how it works. If I am all wet, Coach Uncle Marino will let me know. On the other hand, you may want to research this for yourselves.

The Player Try-Out Camps

The teams require nearly 1,500 players, perhaps more, to field viable professional football teams. Before the draft, all the good college juniors and seniors are invited to a weekend camp affair where they are measured, interviewed, x-rayed, do bench presses, do something called a vertical leap, and run. Running the 40-yard dash in anything under five seconds is a good time.

After watching the players at this event, the coaches are ready to make their picks at the draft. To complete their teams they can trade with another team, they can sign a free agent, or they can find other college kids to hire.

The scouts have been scouring the nation's colleges for more players than the sweet ones acknowledged as good enough to be selected in the draft. Some teams hold try-out camps where all these other eligible, interested, invited young players come together for a few days to try out with a given team. The hopeful players do all the things required at the college draft camp, and they play ball. If one or two or more of these visitors to try-outs interest the coaches, they are offered what might be considered a minimum wage and signed on with the team.

I wish I had a success story to regale you with about a player who was not selected in the draft but hired outright from one of these try-out sessions, but I do not have one. It certainly would be interesting. As part of your business of being a fan, you may want to ascertain how your team selected and signed your favorite players to see if they came from these humble beginnings.

CHAPTER 8

GRADUATION~ ~
LET'S SEE A FOOTBALL GAME

F or three weekends beginning in late December, the NFL play-off games are held. During the last weeks of the regular 16 game season, prior to the play-offs, the football gurus of the air make every effort to keep the fan apprised of the standings of different teams; who has secured a play-off birth and who has not. The team with the best win/loss record in each of the divisions automatically gets a spot even though there may be other teams that have better records in other divisions. (See Table of NFL Teams, Chapter 2.)

The next tier consists of the three teams in the conference with the best win/loss records who were not first in their divisions. These spots are called wild card places. There are, therefore, 12 of the 30 NFL teams participating in the play-offs, six in each conference. The complexity of the whole thing arises from the fact that one team's spot can be contingent on the outcome of the games of several other teams. To make matters even more complex, the best teams get what is called "home field advantage" and this changes as the weeks go buy. All this playing off ends up with champions in each of the American and National Football Con-ferences, who meet each other in the Super Bowl. Even though I'm giving it just a page, you should know that there are a million stories in this aspect of professional football, enough to fill my next book.

In 1996, the 30th Super Bowl will be held, as always, on the last Sunday in January. Though it was not always the case, these events are now held at stadiums in the warmer climates such as in Florida or California and have the largest viewing audience of any TV event in the year. The hosts of the occasion begin planning it months or years in advance. There is always a fabulous Hollywood-style half-time show with stars and celebrities and local marching bands and drill teams. It is a grand spectacle and fun to be part of.

I began this book by telling you that one of the reasons to learn about football was so you could go to some swell Super Bowl party and actually have an opinion about who will win and most certainly understand what is happening in the game. I want to en-courage you to participate in all the fun. Don't be left out. Con-sider it part of your graduation. On the other hand, don't wait for the end of the season, go to a game now!

Let's Go Out To The Ball Game

Now you know a few of the basics that keep the game going on the field. You have selected your favorite team and you know how it has acquired its players. Now it's time to graduate into being a full fledged FAN. Invite your husband or man friend to "take you out to the ball game, take you out to the crowd," oh, you know. He'll probably fall over in a faint unless you've been sharing your fannish pursuit with him all along. And he'll be pleased. Of course, you can also stay home and watch the games on TV. Many people prefer watching on TV because the game can actually be seen better. Instant replays and the commentary of the broadcasters make the game very interesting. And sometimes it's just more comfortable in your own living room with your own refrigerator close at hand. However, at least once, you should attend a game in person.

As I have repeatedly said, every town, small or large, has a Friday night or Saturday afternoon football game. You can choose to attend a game of Pop Warner, high school, junior college, college or professional football. You must understand that while the basic game is essentially the same for all, each level has different rules. If you learn the basics, however, you can choose to be a fan at any level.

Some people are bored to death with a college game, and are only interested in watching the few fine athletes who make it to the NFL. Some fans are not in the least interested in professional football because it's too commercial and too 'big time'. They attend only the local high school football games where they know the players because they live next door. If you go to the games near home, no advice is needed, just follow the crowd. Attending a professional football game may be confusing, though, and you may need a preview of what to expect.

Attending An NFL Game

Buy your tickets well ahead of time. Some big games get sold out early. Go to a ticket agency or call the stadium to reserve your seats with your credit card. They will mail them or keep them for you at a WILL CALL window that will be easy to locate. See, just like a concert!

What to wear? In the old days, women went stylin' to the stadium in their high heels, fur coats, and fancy hats. There was an element of glamour attached to the occasion which is now sort of passé. Start with checking the weather. By gar, did I tell you that the season goes from late August to late January. Yes, I believe I did. Sixteen regular games. So, depending on where you live and the time of the year, and yet again, the weather, dress comfortably. Some stadiums are covered, some are not. Nonetheless, this is an outdoor, sort of active, activity.

It will be easier for you to get into the game if you wear easy clothes. In California, of course, where easy clothes are the accepted way, this is, er, easy. In the east where there is a more formal life-style, people usually dress more formally. Oh, well. Start a trend. Be comfortable, be informal in Philadelphia or New York. Wear a jogging or warm-up suit or jeans, a warm sweater and tennis shoes to the stadium. Layers that may be removed or added might be the best idea. Lest we get too concerned about what to wear, mostly the people there will be looking at the game rather than being critical of your ensemble.

You might wish to bring a pillow sit-upon for the tush. Sometimes a three hour game can do terrible things to one's derriere. And binoculars make things more fun. Forget the camera, there is no one to take a picture of except you and your date and you can do that later at home.

Don't try to lug along too many things because you will be worn out with the experience before it's actually begun. Leave the majority of items that create your comfort zone at home. Some people like to sneak in a bottle of booze. However, it's much better to forget the booze and buy whatever you need to eat or drink at the game. A ball game is the only place in the world where hot dogs really taste good, and health food is unheard of here in this foreign place. So, get ready for a fun day of snacking and eating junk food, something you would not otherwise allow yourself.

The trek from the car or the bus can be a long one. Unless, of course, you wish to really celebrate your new-found avocation and your graduation to fannishness, and you want to hire a limo for the occasion. You will be surprised at the large numbers of stretch limos assembled near the entrances to the big stadium. Yes indeed, on thinking it over, this is definitely the way to go. Hire a limo!

There are attendants everywhere on the grounds. They can tell you exactly where to go and how to find your seat. Buy a program as you enter.

The Scoreboard

One of the first things to do after you find your seat and get settled in is to locate the scoreboard. If you've already forgotten all that you learned in this book, the scoreboard offers quite a good bit of information. For one thing, how much longer you will be needing to sit here. The scoreboard keeps track of the time for the spectators - you know, for the fans.

Another thing you can determine from the scoreboard is what the current score is and who's ahead of whom in the game. Usually you will see the words **HOME** and **VISITOR** in large lighted letters on the board. **HOME** refers to the team that usually plays in this stadium, the home team. It's nice to figure out the score this way if you can't tell by watching yourself.

Scoreboards in big stadiums also have humongous TV screens that show instant replays (of plays on the field), pictures, statistics, even words to songs to be sung. You can also tell what down (remember, which try) it is and how far the team in possession of the ball needs to go for a first down.

So, you're here. You will be taken aback by the roar of the crowd. Your first time at the stadium may be a little overwhelming because of the noise. But the noise is part of the drama and after awhile, you will begin to get into it yourself and find that noise very exciting.

The Field

In the trailers for a recent popular movie, Gena Davis says, "Astro turf or grass. Who cares?" The implication is that only men would care about such inconsequential folly. The fact is, this is one of the most critical issues in pro football. Astro turf is a kind of fake, plastic grass. It does not have the same elasticity and give as real turf or grass, and has been the cause of many serious injuries. Ask any player. None will say he prefers to play on astro turf.

The astro turf experiment came about for several reasons. The primary one being that real turf is difficult to grow indoors. The name is derivative of the Astro Dome, one of the first covered stadiums, located in Houston, Texas. Several other stadiums are essentially roofed. The care and feeding of astro turf is not as expensive as caring for real grass, and the team owners look to ways to cut costs. Unfortunately, it seems this is a way to be penny wise and pound foolish. The injuries to players can be very expensive. Every year, some stadiums convert back to grass. Every year, fans, coaches and players hope for the end of astro turf.

See Your Team

Locating your team should not be all that difficult inasmuch as there are only two teams on the field. You should, by now, know the colors of your team's jerseys. Find your special players by their numbers. While they're on the field, you'll not be able to recognize them other than by the large numerals on the backs of their jerseys and if you're seated close enough, by their last names printed there as well.

The players carry a huge amount of gear and paraphernalia designed to protect them from injury, many pounds worth. The paraphernalia consists of huge shoulder pads, thigh pads, some rib protection, private part cups, all kinds of braces and wrappings around knees, hands, wrists, legs and arms. Each player has a special configuration of protective devices designed especially for him. The efficiency of the protective paraphernalia is constantly being improved upon.

The helmets carry the team logo and have a variety of face guards, from a single bar to multiple bars, sun shade glass and so on. You cannot use faces to identify where your best guy is, except when he takes off his helmet, when he's on the sideline, not playing. We're glad for all this protection; in the melee that you're about to witness, you'll fear for the safety of your heros. The elaborate attire helps keep them from getting injured.

Take some time to read the program that you purchased when you first arrived. It contains pictures and stories about the players along with their numbers, age, height, weight and usually the college where they played football. There also may be other stories that would be interesting to fans. Some programs show pictures of the officials' signals that we talked about in Chapter 6 that are used by the referees to let the crowd know what is happening. The programs also contain advertisements of all sorts; you may read these if you like or these you may ignore - after all, you paid for this program so you don't need to be sympathetic to the advertisers who want you to buy this stuff.

Look for the officials on the field. You will remember that they wear black and white striped shirts, white knickers, and black baseball caps, except the Referee who wears a white one. They also have letters on their backs telling which official they are. Like 'R' for Referee. Watching them will keep you in touch with the game as it progresses. Do you see the ones we described in day-glo orange on the sidelines? Look for the chain gang, the officials who keep the down markers and the 10-yard-long chain to keep track of the downs.

See if you can identify the coaches for both teams. Remember our discussion about how they dressed?

The Revelry

There is much whoopla associated with professional football, many props and mascots and souvenirs. The Pittsburgh Steeler fans have 'terrible towels', gold ones that they wave throughout the game when they are encouraging their team to score or when the team has just scored. They also support their defensive squad by waving their towels.

The San Diego Chargers have a cannon that is shot off when the team scores. John Madden, the former coach turned broadcaster, had some interesting comments about the charm of the Chargers' cannon. The USC Trojans have the Trojan horse prancing about on the sidelines. Of course, we know, that's college. Most teams have a mascot, either a person dressed up in a costume that characterizes the mascot, like a bear or some other animal, or they have the real thing, like a Bengal Tiger in Cincinnati.

Notice the young women, cheerleaders, on the sidelines. Quite a departure, huh, from the heavy sweaters, pleated skirts and saddle shoes of other times and places. Their routines are entertaining and they've worked hard to perfect them. You will enjoy watching their enthusiasm, and you'll watch the men watching them. You may have some feelings about this aspect of the day at the stadium.

There is always music, you know, "dah, dah, dah, dat, ta, dah... CHARGE," that sort of thing. Some stadiums have great sound systems where jazz is piped through. Others have a wonderful loud organ and others have a small sports band. All fun and festive adding to the delight of the day.

You'll like it, you really will. But you must be relaxed and open to the experience of the occasion. There is much to see and much to comprehend. The time will go by very rapidly in most cases. When you're at home and not involved, it seems for some like profes-sional football games are interminable. At the stadium, there is so much going on that the time will go quickly by. Besides, you'll be so thrilled to be in close proximity to your new heros, you'll be disap-pointed when the game is over.

Going to the stadium makes it all so much more real. Bigger than life. The TV screen and radio coverage diminish the proceedings and make them somehow appear less than they are. Watched at home, the players seem distant, actors in an unreal movie. A trip to the stadium puts it in perspective. These are real people, these players, real young men. The LA Coliseum holds 65,000 people. That's a good-sized city. The noise these 65,000 individuals make along with the bands and organs and announcers is unimaginable. Bigger than life, the energy astonishing. A divertissement, a pleasure, a real adventure.

Now you have become an indisputably genuine fan. You can avoid the cynicism that easily creeps into a discussion about professional football. You can accept it and allow the players to play, inasmuch as that's what they have chosen to do. You can understand that for some people, life is difficult, and loving a team, whether watched on TV or at the stadium, removes them from that difficult life for awhile. And you, too. Just go with the flow. Allow the event to unfold as it will. Get into it with the others that love the game. Be a FAN. Enjoy.

Bibliography

Akers, John. "Bay Area Players Won't Go High In Draft." *San Jose Mercury News*. p.C1. April 15, 1995.

Brantingham, Barney. *Pro Football Hall of Fame: The Story Behind the Dream*. Sequoia Communications for The Football Hall of Fame. 1988.

Cunningham, Randall. *I'm Still Scrambling*. Bantam Doubleday Dell Publishing Group. New York. 1993.

Dreayer, Barry. *Teach Me Sports: Join The Fun By Learning the Game: Football*. General Publishing Group, Inc. Santa Monica, CA. 1994.

Foehr, Donna. *Football For Women: And Men Who Want To Learn The Game*. National Press, Inc. Bethesda, Maryland. 1988.

Gifford, Frank; Waters, Harry. *The Whole Ten Yards*. Random House, Inc. New York. 1993.

Graves, Ray. *Ray Graves' Guide to Modern Football Offense*. Parker Publishing. New York. 1967.

Herskowitz, Mickey. *The Quarterbacks: The Uncensored Truth About Men in the Pocket*. William Morrow and Co., Inc. New York. 1990.

Hollander, Zander, Editor. *1994-The Complete Handbook of Pro Football*. Signet. 1994.

Judge, Clark. "Moore Headed to 49ers." *San Jose Mercury News*. p.C1. April 15, 1994.

Markbreit, Jerry. *The Armchair Referee: 500 Questions and Answers About Football*. Doubleday and Company. New York. 1973.

Montville, Leigh. "Forward Progress: In 75 years the NFL has become a technological colossus." *Sports Illustrated*. p. 26. Vol.81. No.10. Sept.5, 1994.

Nadel, John. "Kaufman a No.1 Hit With Raiders." *Santa Barbara News Press*. p.C1. April 23, 1995.

"NFL Draft Preview." *Inside Sports*. p. 28. Vol.17. No.5. May, 1995.

"NFL Playoff Preview." *Inside Sports*. p.28 - 36. Vol.17. No.1. January, 1995.

"NFL Preview '94." *Sports Illustrated*. Vol 81. No.10. Sept 5, 1994.

NFL's 75th Anniversary Issue. *Pro Football Weekly*. Vol. 9. No.4. Sept. 1994.

Price, S.L. "The Long View." *Sports Illustrated*. p.40. Vol.81. No.9. Aug.29, 1994.

1994 Season in Review. *Pro Football Weekly*. Vol 9. No. 29. April 1995.

Riggins, John; Winter, Jack. *Gameplan: The Language and Strategy of Pro Football*. Santa Barbara Press. Santa Barbara, CA. 1984.

"Viewers'Guide to the NFL." *TV Guide*. Fall, 1994.

Whittingham, Richard, Editor. *The Fireside Book of Pro Football: An anthology of the best, most entertaining writing about professional football, featuring: Frank Defore et.al.* A Fireside Book, Simon & Schuster Inc. New York.1989

Zant, John. "Look Out L.A., Here Comes Nip." *Santa Barbara News Press*. p.C1. April 23, 1995.

INDEX

ERRATA: Page numbers for INDEX entries are off by 2. To find the correct page number, subtract 2, e.g. Astro Dome, p.130 minus 2 = p.128.

free-agency 113, 122, 123, 124
frequency chart 63
front line 35, 52, 53, 57, 58, 77, 78,
   79
front office 61
fullback 52
fumble 59
G
Galloway, Joey 118
game plan 63, 78
gear131
goal 44, 65, 69
goal line 42, 44, 49, 51, 54, 64, 66,
   91, 95, 103, 111
goal posts 42, 50, 91
golf 16, 17
Graves, Ray 77
Green Bay Packers 32
Green, Kevin 35
groupies 24, 35, 36
guard 52, 54, 55, 56, 57, 78, 83, 91,
   95, 108
H
half 50, 65, 67, 68, 104, 111
halfback 52, 53, 56, 57
halfback pass 95
half-time 40
hand-off 83, 92
hash marks 42
Heisman Trophy 120, 121
helmet 109, 114, 131
holding 53, 111
hole 58, 76, 77, 78, 79, 83
home field advantage 126
hook 91

Houston Oilers 32, 117
huddle 51, 52, 64, 65, 87, 92
hurdling 92
hurry up offense 65, 66
I
illegal contact 108
illegal man down field 108
illegal motion 106
illegal touching 112
illegal use of hands 108, 110
incomplete pass 66, 103, 105
Indianapolis Colts 32
ineligible reciever 112
instant replay 100, 105, 129
intentional grounding 110
intercept, interception 59
J
Jacksonville Jaguars 32, 116
jerseys 37, 53, 54, 57, 111, 130
Johnson, Vance, Preface
Jones, Brent 20
Judges 104
K
Kalaha 15, 17
Kansas City Chiefs 27, 28, 29, 32,
   118
Kaufman, Napoleon 119, 120
Kiper, Mel Jr. 114, 116, 118, 119
kick 59, 61, 67, 68, 72, 74
kicked 59, 108, 109, 111
kicker 50, 51, 55, 57, 69, 72, 108,
   109
kick off 51, 67, 72, 73, 100, 104
Kotite, Rich 101

touchback51, 67, 69, 72
touchdown, TD 49, 50, 59, 66, 69,
    103, 112
trade 113, 115, 120, 122, 123, 124
tripping 108, 110
try-out camps 113, 124
turnover 29, 59
two minute drill 65, 91
two minute warning 65
U
Umpire 45, 46
unnecessary roughness 108, 109
unsportsmanlike conduct 111, 112
University of Southern California
    (USC) 28, 116, 121, 122, 132
V
veer 79, 81
vertical leap 124
W
waivers 123
war rooms 115
Washington Redskins 20, 32, 114,
    117
weak side 79
Westbrook, Michael 117
Wheatly, Tyrone 119
whistle 104
wide receiver 53, 62, 87, 92, 98,
    117, 118
wild card 125
Williams, Calvin 101, 102
win/loss record 33, 115, 125
Winter, John 78
Wyche, Sam 117

Y
yardage 47, 64, 65, 91, 92, 104
yard line 42, 43, 44, 50, 51, 53
Young, Steve 20, 102
Z
zone defense 98

About The Author

Janet Benner, Ph.D. has spent her career working as an administrator in social service agencies and as a writer. She has written books about parenting, general fitness, and how to quit smoking. She always enjoyed football, playing herself in the large vacant lot next to the house where she grew up. She was regularly one of the first kids in the neighborhood chosen to play, and often was appointed to play quarterback.

It is no different today than when she was a child, young girls were not allowed to play on the organized teams at school or in community leagues. The closest she came was being a cheerleader, directing appreciative fans in cheers and chants expressing the enthusiasm she herself felt for the game of football. The extended career of her brother who was all league his senior year in high school, then received a scholarship to attend USC, helped engender her eagerness.

Ms. Benner eventually married a college boy who, himself was an athlete, and who subsequently became a high school football coach. During their college days, she sat at games with other football wives who seemed not to understand at all what was happening on the field. She happily kept a running commentary to help keep the wives tuned in. Though she and the coach went separate ways, her interest in the game thrived through the years.

The decision to write *Football: Mysteries Revealed* came from all the women Ms. Benner talked to who wanted to know for various reasons, what all the fuss was about.

Other books by Janet Benner include: *Parent Survival Training, a Guide for Parents of Teenagers* and *Smoking Cigarettes: The Unfiltered Truth: Understand Why and How To Quit.*

Ms. Benner lives and works in Santa Barbara, California.

Order Additional Copies

Please send me _____ copies of *Football: Mysteries Revealed for the Feminine Fan: Understanding and Enjoying the Game* to the address below. Total payment in the amount of $_____ * is enclosed.

*1. $14.95 each copy.
 2. In California add 7.75% sales tax for books not for resale.
 3. Please include $1.75 for shipping and handling for the first book, $ .75 for each additional book.
 4. Please discount 40% for orders of three or more copies.

Name _____

Address _____

City _____ State _____ Zip _____

Make checks payable and mail to:

JOELLE PUBLISHING
P.O. BOX 91229
SANTA BARBARA, CA 93190

FAX: 805-965-0332
TELEPHONE: 805-962-9887